NEW ZEALAND
RAILWAYS

Their Life and Times

ROBIN BROMBY

Highgate Publishing
Sydney

[Based on the author's Rails That Built a Nation, published in 2003 by Grantham House, but reformatted with extensive editing and additions]

First published 2014 by Highgate Publishing, P O Box 481, Edgecliff NSW 2027, Australia. (www.highgatepublishing.com.au)

National Library of Australia Cataloguing-in-Publication entry

Creator: Bromby, Robin, 1942- author.

Title: New Zealand railways : their life and times / Robin Bromby.

ISBN: 9780992595609

Notes: Includes bibliographical references.

Subjects: Railroads--New Zealand--History. Railroad travel--New Zealand--History.

Dewey Number: 385.0993

Cover: On a misty mid-morning on 21 May 1969, Ja 1274 pulls out of Milton on the Main South line hauling a Limited Express that began its journey at Invercargill and will by early evening run on to the wharf at Lyttelton to discharge passengers making for Wellington on the overnight ferry. (Wilson Lythgoe)

New Zealand
Railways

Contents

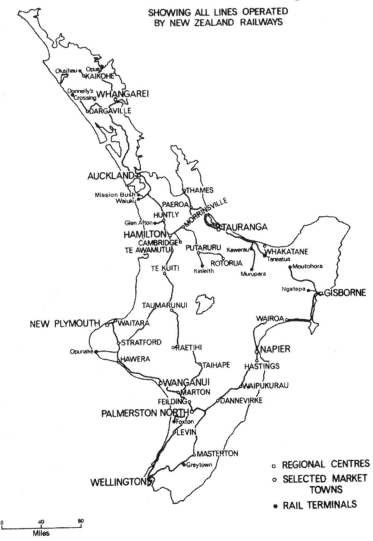

North Island Railways

SHOWING ALL LINES OPERATED
BY NEW ZEALAND RAILWAYS

□ REGIONAL CENTRES
○ SELECTED MARKET
     TOWNS
● RAIL TERMINALS

These maps illustrate the extent of rail building, showing a very complex network for a country with such a low and sparse population. New Zealand did not reach one million people until 1909. By 1945, when the last of the main lines was completed and with most of the branch lines still in existence, the country had just 1.7 million people. (*Maps courtesy of Euan McQueen*)

South Island Railways

SHOWING ALL LINES OPERATED
BY NEW ZEALAND RAILWAYS

NELSON
Picton
Seddonville
Glenhope
BLENHEIM
WESTPORT
Reefton
Roa
Rapahoe
GREYMOUTH
Waiau
Ross
West Oxford
Rangiora
Whitecliffs
CHRISTCHURCH
Methven
Springburn
Southbridge
Little River
ASHBURTON
Fairlie
TIMARU
WAIMATE
Kurow
Ngapara
Tokarahi
OAMARU
Cromwell
Dunback
Makareao
Kingston
Roxburgh
Mossburn
Waikaia
Edievale
DUNEDIN
Ohai
Waikaka
Outram
Wairio
GORE
Orawia
Hedgehope
BALCLUTHA
Wyndham
Glenham
Tahakopa
INVERCARGILL
Tokanui
Bluff

□ REGIONAL CENTRES
○ SELECTED MARKET TOWNS
● RAIL TERMINALS

0   40   80
Miles

Introduction

NEW ZEALAND'S RAILWAY SYSTEM was at its greatest length of 5,656 km until, on 5 December 1953, the Outram branch near Dunedin was closed. The branch, 14.5 km in length, serving only one small settlement and running almost its entire length through farmland, was one of many rural lines in New Zealand that owed their existence to local political interests. Landowners, in order to win their case for a railway, had offered to make land available free of charge provided trains ran six days a week. The line opened to traffic on 1 October 1877. By the early 1950s, however, the branch's economics were typical of many rural lines. Passenger services had ended in 1950 and in its last years the only goods traffic of note was the cartage of lime and fertiliser. Average weekly freight amounted to 107 tons inwards, just seven tons outwards. On average, sheep and cattle transport on the line amounted to twenty-three head a week. In 1951 the Outram branch lost £5,056, a figure almost double its revenue. On top of that, New Zealand Railways (NZR) determined that £16,000 needed to be spent on new sleepers to keep the line safe for trains. The end was thus inevitable.

Within weeks of Outram seeing its last revenue train, other lines were shut down: the Waihao Downs-Waimate section in South Canterbury, the Browns-Hedgehope section in Southland and the Greytown branch in Wairarapa. The Eyreton branch in North Canterbury was closed a few months later, in May 1954.

* * *

Wf 398 (2-6-4T) seen here in January 1947 in a quiet Greytown yard: the carriage and brake van that made up the train to Woodside, just 5km away on the main line to Wellington, sit at the passenger platform. There are no goods wagons in sight. The short branch was one of the first victims of the 1953 closures. (*Wairarapa Archive*)

The pattern was clear. The era of railways as the mainstay of land transport throughout New Zealand was ending. One by one, most of the rural branches would disappear over the next forty years; the ones that survived the longest would be those serving bulk traffic, such as logs on the Dargaville branch in North Auckland and coal on the Wairio branch in Southland.

There were some rays of hope in the years immediately following the Second World War. In his annual Railways Statement to Parliament in 1950, Minister of Railways William Gooseman announced that revenue for the year to March was the highest yearly figure ever for New Zealand Railways (or NZR as it was usually called): £19.54 million. Passenger revenues were also up mainly because the department was able to put more first class and sleeping cars back into service after the war, along with the restoration of the daylight expresses between Auckland and Wellington (supplementing the overnight trains) and the running of special trains for the Empire Games held in Auckland that year. The annual loss had been cut to £1.05 million.

But Gooseman signalled that the years of government indulgence were over. After fourteen years of Labour government and its widening of state-owned activities in the economy, the more free-enterprise oriented National Party had come to power in November 1949 and the new minister made it clear to Parliament that 'the government considers it proper that those who avail themselves of the services provided by the railways should pay for them'.

In 1953, the government moved to close those lines that were without hope of paying their way.

Non-paying lines were as old as the railway system itself. That was all very well when there were few alternatives to rail, but as soon as road was able to offer cheaper and usually faster transport times (particularly over the shorter distances), then that was another matter. In 1926 the NZR chief accountant, Mr H. Valentine, said it was the non-paying branch lines that were the main factor responsible for the parlous state of railway finances. Twenty-eight branches were so classed and together they earned NZR £258,243 against their £541,710 combined deficit once their share of interest charges plus expenditure were added together. And that calculation allowed a credit of £36,568 for their assessed value as feeders; that is, the traffic they generated that would go on to earn revenue on main line services. Those lines covered a combined 1,245 km. There were exceptions, and Valentine drew attention to two branches that actually paid their way: Waitara in Taranaki and Foxton in Manawatu. The total cost (operating expenses and interest) was £23,044 but their revenue (£14,265) plus an allowance for feeder value of £14,273, left these earning a combined profit of £5,494. That these lines, together, covered only 40 km between them showed that a branch did not need to be long to be economic; they just had to serve the right places and have a demand for their use. Too many branches did not and, indeed, both Foxton and Waitara would once more subside into the red and be closed.

The last days of a branch line. Here A 601 is seen at Himatangi on the Foxton branch three months before the line's closure on 18 July 1959, the locomotive with one wagon attached standing at the goods shed. (*B Poulson – Bob Stott Collection*)

In 1931 the Chicago Tribune published a long article, 'Railway Luxury Hits Taxpayers in New Zealand'. Filed from Wellington on 6 December, the report noted that 'the story of New Zealand railroads furnishes one of the best examples of the inefficiency of a state built on the theories prevalent here'. Over the previous four years, NZR had failed by more than the equivalent of $US10 million to cover just its interest bill, let alone operating costs. The article described the South Island as the 'graveyard of the railway system' with a long trunk line running down the east coast and branch lines off it running toward the mountain range, looking like one half of a fish skeleton. 'These lines, pushed on against all prudence or considerations of return, have been the downfall of the railway system, for they had laid on it a burden from which it has never escaped'.

Branch losses 1936

(Later name changes in parentheses. * indicates profit)

	Length (km)	Net loss (in £)
North Island		
Kaikohe (Okaihau)	40	5,218
Kirikopuni (Dargaville)	22.5	2,646
Waiuku	21	59*
Taneatua (East Coast Main Trunk)	178.5	3,426
Opunake	37	4,316
Greytown	5	1,212
South Island		
Eyreton and Oxford branches	69	6,973
Cheviot (Main North)	70.5	8,102
Little River	37	4,470
Southbridge	49	794*
Whitecliffs	19	357
Methven	35.5	830
Springburn (Mt Somers)	43	802

	Length (km)	Net loss (in £)
Fairlie	58	563
Waimate	13.5	1,117
Kurow	59.5	2,254
Ngapara	24	212
Waihemo (Dunback)	14.5	378*
Otago Central	23	61,334
Outram	14.5	1,425
Roxburgh	95	4,796
Catlins River	68.5	3,462
Tapanui	42.5	83
Waikaka	21	352*
Switzers (Waikaia)	22	97
Wyndham	6.5	111
Seaward Bush	54.5	320
Mararoa (Mossburn)	16.5	933

Isolated Sections

Kaihu	38.5	2,775
Gisborne (Moutohora Branch)	78	4,046
Nelson	103	5,232
Picton (Main North)	90	456*

Note: Figures do not include interest charges. For example, the £4,046 loss on the Gisborne section became £37,065 once interest was added

* * *

The Chicago Tribune article cited a special commission of 1926 (presumably the Fay Raven Commission which reported in 1925) which recorded 'with astonishment' there were no reserve funds set aside for the depreciation of the NZR system.

The Great Depression took its toll not only on the revenue needed for the running of the rail system, but the savage cuts in government spending hindered development of the network. In October 1930 the New Zealand Herald reported on languishing rail projects. Three lines on which work had been proceeding for several years had suddenly had their worked stopped as the coalition government under Prime Minister George Forbes slashed spending. The most notable one to be halted concerned what was the missing link in the national trunk system, on what would become the Main North line (Christchurch to Picton) in the northern section of the South Island. There was a 118 km gap between Wharanui (reached in 1915) and Parnassus (reached in 1912). The gap would not be closed until 1945.

Another key main line project to be halted was a 54 km section of what was planned as the Napier-Gisborne railway. The section from Putorino to Wairoa would not be handed over to NZR until 1939. The third disappointment involved building a section through the difficult Buller Gorge to link the isolated sections centred on Westport with Nelson. Work had begun on this section before the First World War but was abandoned in 1915; construction started again in 1926. Now work ground to a halt yet again (and the connection with the Nelson line would never be completed). In the far north of New Zealand, the government cancelled work on an extension to the Okai-hau branch, to take the line on to a new terminus at Rangiahua, a project on which 221 men were working at the time; that section would never be opened. Another 145 men had lost their jobs when work stopped on the section to link the isolated Kaihu branch, also in the far north, to the national system, although work on that would be completed in 1943.

Fortunately for New Zealand's railway system, 1935 saw the election of the country's first Labour government with its very positive attitude toward rail. By the time of the presentation of the 1936 annual report, the new minister was able to tell Parliament that work has been stepped up throughout the system including the improvement of lavatories in ninety-four carriages and installation of lavatories in thirteen existing carriages. In addition, sixty-one carriages were being upgraded to include steam heating (that is, hot water piped through the train from the locomotive), thirty-five cars were being given centre partitions with doors, and fifty-one cars were being stripped of the old longitudinal seating, that being replaced with forward facing seats. Apart from the Rangiahua extension and the connection of Nelson to the main NZR network, all the stalled rail extensions left over from the United-Reform coalition government would be re-started and completed before Labour left office in 1949.

I

In 1953 anyone trying to predict the future fifty years on, the present KiwiRail system — as the state-owned railway network is known — of today would have been barely imaginable. Who back then might have considered a railway system in 2014 which comprised a relatively few main lines, with almost all rural branches closed, the central section of the North Island Main Trunk electrified, and a railway system largely dependent on bulk traffic with long coal, log and milk trains speeding along on bogie wagons? So many of the familiar parts of the railway in 1953 have now disappeared forever: refreshment rooms, sidings and goods sheds at a myriad of small stations each only a few miles from the other.

Outside the main centres with their suburban lines, it is getting hard to spot any of those magnificent old station buildings with their waiting room, the departure bell and verandah to protect passengers from the elements. Those which have survived have managed to so by becoming tourist or craft centres (the terminus station on the Little River branch, for example) or because a local group has fought to save them (Ormondville in Hawke's Bay is a prime example) — but not, alas, the magnificent wooden station at Ashburton, south of Christchurch, demolished in 2013.

In 1953, the year in which New Zealand's railways reached their zenith in terms of route mileage, NZR employed 25,000 people. Diesel-electric traction was being introduced, but steam was still king; indeed, that year saw two new Ja steam locomotives placed in service in the South Island. But the tide was turning. While there were a further seven Ja locomotives on the order books, NZR had also contracted for forty-one main-line diesel-electric locomotives and fifty-eight diesel-mechanical shunting engines.

The thirty-mile (48.2 km) limit still applied, banning road operators moving any freight over that distance if a rail line existed over the same route. The average railway goods haul was just eighty miles (128.5km) in the South Island, 129 miles (207 km) in the North Island.

In the year to March 1954 NZR recorded 1.82 million more passenger journeys than in the previous year, most of this 8.5 per cent increase being due to the introduction of the electric multiple units based at Wellington to serve the fast growing suburbs of the Hutt Valley across the harbour from the capital.

Parcels, luggage (including left luggage, checked luggage, bicycles, dogs and newspapers) and mail were still important sources of income, bringing NZR £600,497, out of total revenue of £27.9 million.

The far-flung NZR empire included the steamer *Earnslaw*, based in the inland town of Queenstown, serving isolated farms and settlements dotted around the vast Lake Wakatipu (and still running today as a popular tourist attraction); there were refreshment rooms (although 1953 saw the closure of rooms at Napier, Otira and Waipara in North Canterbury), bookstalls, and railway houses and huts dotted around the country, as well as suburban and long-distance NZR road services buses.

Stock transport — now a thing of the past — back in 1953 represented 16.1 per cent of all goods traffic, but coal was by far the single largest source of freight revenue, with 24.8 per cent of the total. The wagon fleet included ninety-nine horseboxes, 4,454 cattle and sheep wagons and 1,327 coal hoppers out of a total 33,763 four-wheel wagons. There were another 2,967 bogie wagons, of which 450 carried chilled or frozen meat. NZR owned 1,363 carriages (15 sleeping and 1,115 second-class cars among them), 127 electric multiple unit motor cars and trailers, eight postal vans, 461 brake vans, twenty-one railcars and 718 locomotives.

Operationally, the highlights of 1953-54 were the Royal tour and the special train assembled to transport Queen Elizabeth II and the Duke of Edinburgh around the country, along with the introduction of electric suburban services between Wellington and Taita, and the increase in express passenger train services between Wellington-New Plymouth and Auckland-Opua. However, timekeeping by all expresses on the NZR system was rather dismal, with only forty per cent of trains arriving on time at main towns and terminus stations. The situation was worse in the North Island because of congestion on the main lines and the large number of temporary speed restrictions.

Since then, the New Zealand railway system has seemed to many as having lost much of its glory. New Zealand Railways once operated 1,350 railway stations; by the beginning of the twenty-first century, fewer than 100 remained open, although one new one has been opened: the Britomart Transport Centre in downtown Auckland. Obviously, the system could not be preserved in aspic, but one sometimes had a feeling that, to those guiding the system, the only good railway line was a closed one. While branch lines lost money, some also generated traffic that provided additional revenue when moving along the trunk lines.

It was a pity, in retrospect, that the various governments and NZR administrators did not adopt the more relaxed style of Australia, where marginal or loss-making lines were quietly mothballed but often left intact, so that they could always be reopened should traffic pick up again — a point reinforced by the subsequent development of commercial forests in areas once served by branch lines; the Moutohora branch in Poverty Bay and the Okaihau branch in Northland were the most obvious examples.

A Note Regarding Currency

New Zealand in 1967 switched from using pounds, shillings and pence, to decimal currency (dollars and cents). A pound was made up of twenty shillings, a shilling of twelve pence — making a pound comprised of 240 pence. So far as this book is concerned, the old currency will be rendered thus: fifteen pounds, two shillings and six pence will appear as £15 2s 6d. Because of the vastly inflated value of money today, converting amounts into dollars of today makes no sense.

1
Heyday

Top passenger stations 1950

The stations selling the most passenger tickets in fiscal 1950 were:

Wellington	1,101,656
Auckland	617,066
Christchurch	536,124
Dunedin	344,057
Petone	297,265
Lyttelton	152,151
Greymouth	147,685
Palmerston North	142,198
Papakura	132,044
Invercargill	109,841
Otahuhu	103,208

Stations selling fewest tickets that year (with line location in parenthesis):

Runanga (Rewanui)	2
Glenhope (Nelson)	45
Ealing (Main South)	75
Mt Somers (Mt Somers)	95
Waikari (Main North)	99
Hawarden (Waiau)	109
Waiau (Waiau)	109
Miller's Flat (Roxburgh)	134

(All those in the second category were in the South Island.)

THE GREATEST NUMBER OF passengers carried in any financial year was recorded in 1943-44, not surprising given petrol rationing during the Second World War. However, the numbers dropped away substantially in the years after the war. Apart from the coal and staff shortages that caused cancellations and reductions of many long-distance services, the number of troop movements fell away and gradually more people acquired their own cars. By the 1960s few children still used trains to get to and from school with buses having taken over most of that task.

The decline was further hastened by closure of branch lines and withdrawal of mixed trains on the surviving lines. By 1970 most of the old wooden carriages had been scrapped by NZR, but there was no programme to build additional steel cars.

Furthermore, from the 1920s NZR was to turn increasingly to road services with the establishment of the New Zealand

Railway Road Services. The first bus working under NZR appeared as early as 1907, when a service ran between the railhead at Culverden in North Canterbury to Waiau. In 1926 NZR purchased the bus service between Napier and Hastings, then over 1927-28 acquired operations in the Hutt Valley and began Lower Hutt-Wellington services. By 1934 NZRRS had moved into long-distance bus operations, with buses operating between Wellington and Wanganui.

The growth was spectacular. In 1930 NZRRS owned sixty buses; by 1965 the fleet numbered 787 (212 suburban vehicles, 593 long-distance coaches). Between 1936 and 1951 NZRRS operations grew to cover 9,635 route kilometres. In 1965 it owned twenty per cent of New Zealand's buses and operated twenty-five per cent of bus mileage. Its suburban services were many: in Auckland, Hastings and the Hutt Valley near Wellington, NZRRS ran complex route systems. In the last mentioned, for example, buses ran out of Petone and Lower Hutt for a wide variety of destinations: Upper Hutt, Te Marua, Taita, Naenae, Moera and Wainuiomata among them. NZRRS operated a suburban fleet out of Wellington, too, to destinations as far apart as Khandallah and Titahi Bay. There were also some services around Dunedin, including to Mosgiel.

By 1980 the Railway Road Services branch was responsible for 19.8 million journeys. The rail situation was not quite so rosy: suburban rail journeys had fallen to fifteen million while long-distance journeys had shrivelled to 999,000.

While motor transport — the private ownership of cars and the greater flexibility of buses — played an enormous role in changing the whole transport scene in New Zealand, part of the failure of rail since the mid-1970s has been due to lack of imagination. Just as city councils ran their bus operations along former tram routes, so NZR and its successor, Tranz Rail, persisted with 1950s passenger thinking. The Southerner between Christchurch and Invercargill, for example, ran effectively to the same timetable in 2001 as the old Limited services in the 1950s, the latter being timed to coordinate with the inter-island ferries running between Lyttelton and Wellington, a service that vanished in 1976. Flexibility on the rail system dwindled with the withdrawal of services; no longer does a passenger from Dunedin have the choice of the 12.21 pm Southerner or the 5.45pm railcar to get to Christchurch. Now the only passenger trains running in the South Island are essentially tourism operations.

There seems little question that the running down of passenger rail hastened its own demise. A new generation of travellers has grown up without the desire or need to use trains; thus the same Southerner which might have consisted of eight cars in 1980 was down to two on most days by the end of its life.

By contrast, where new thinking has emerged and trains have been designed for tourism, with the journey seen as part of the holiday experience, trains have proved a success — as the TranzAlpine and Coastal Pacific (in the South Island) and Northern Explorer (Auckland-Wellington) have demonstrated.

As for road services, in July 1991 the New Zealand Railways Corporation sold its long-distance operations (by now called InterCity) to private interests.

II

'At Morrinsville Station—Traffic Handled in One Year' was the title of a short piece appearing in the 1 May 1932 issue of *The New Zealand Railways Magazine*, NZR's public relations outreach to the public. In those days, twenty-five trains a day passed through this station in the Waikato section of the East Coast Main Trunk; it was also the junction with the Rotorua branch. There were twelve men employed in the station itself (of which six were clerical staff working shifts) along with twelve track maintenance workers.

The statistics for the year include 21,000 passenger tickets sold, an average of seventy each weekday. Despatched from Morrinsville's yard over the year were 140,000 head of livestock and 14,500 tons of goods; inward traffic totalled 57,000 head of livestock and 33,000 tons of goods (including 10,000 tons of manure and 1.42 million feet of timber). Trains also collected livestock from the nearby flag stations of Kiwitahi, Walton and Tatuanui. According to the article, Morrinsville was second-placed in the North Island in terms of the cattle and calves handled (beaten only by Normanby in Taranaki, which also served an extensive dairying district).

The magazine said a supply of wagons was always kept in the sidings so that a request for rolling stock from stations on the Rotorua and Thames lines could be met promptly.

III

A glimpse of the comprehensive service offered by NZR even in the sparsely populated South Island was given by an incident that led to the arrest in 1895 of Minnie Dean, who gained notoriety when exposed as a baby farmer. She was the first, and only, woman ever to be executed in New Zealand, being hanged at Invercargill gaol.

As recounted during her trial in Invercargill, a railway guard had noticed her boarding a train with a young baby and carrying a hatbox. The same guard was around when she returned with only the hatbox and one that was heavy at that. Dean had travelled by NZR train from her home at Winton (on the Kingston branch) as far as Lumsden where she stayed overnight, having killed the infant, Eva Hornsby, during the journey. The next morning she caught the train across the Waimea Plains branch to Gore, where she transferred to the Dunedin express on the Main South line, alighting at the small station of Milburn. She then collected another infant there, and boarded the next train heading for Dunedin, but again alighting at a wayside station, Clarendon, just north of Milburn. She then smothered the second child, Dorothy Carter, with laudanum. Then Minnie Dean waited at Clarendon for a southbound train, retracing her journey to Gore, then across the Waimea Plains line and then home to Winton along the Kingston branch. Eventually police, who had Dean under observation before this last journey, arrived at her property and dug up the garden to find both the recently deceased infants and the skeleton of another child. The defence lawyer, Alfred Hanlon, later wrote:

> Imagine a being with the name and appearance of a woman boldly using a public railway train for the destruction of her helpless victim, sitting serene and unperturbed in a carriage with one tiny corpse in a tin box at her feet and another enshrouded in a shawl and secured by travelling straps in the luggage rack at her head.

In Dean's day and, indeed, up until variously the 1930s through to the 1950s, a passenger boarding an Invercargill-bound express at Christchurch could take their pick of stations at which they could choose to alight and wait for a local train along a branch line: Rakaia (Methven branch), Tinwald (Mt Somers branch), Timaru (Fairlie branch), Studholme Junction (Waimate branch), Oamaru (Kurow branch), Palmerston (Dunback branch), Dunedin (Otago Central branch), Mosgiel (Outram branch), Milton (Roxburgh branch) Balclutha (Catlins River branch), Waipahi (Tapanui branch), and Gore (Waimea Plains line and Waikaka branch), and then Invercargill itself, where passenger trains departed to serve the Bluff line, Seaward Bush, Kingston and Tuatapere branches.

IV

Now just an unmarked point on the Dunedin-Oamaru section of the Main South line, the small station of Waianakarua was well known to travellers in the 1930s and 1940s as the crossing place for main line expresses. In 1972 *Rails* magazine was running a series called 'Steam Express' in which rail enthusiast J. D.

Mahoney painted word pictures of scenes long disappeared from the world of New Zealand train running. One of those recalled how Train No. 174 from Dunedin was scheduled to arrive at 1.54 pm, stopping outside the home signal until ushered into the loop by the tablet porter. That porter would then close the points, cycle back to the station and put the tablet taken from the driver into the machine. At 1.58 pm Train No. 145 from Oamaru was scheduled to

> roll through on the main line, a kaleidoscope of black steel, steam, gleaming red enamel car sides, vestibules, windows, rows of seats, and hundreds of passengers riding smoothly and assuredly just a few feet from where you were sitting in the waiting train. In a few seconds it would all be over. Soon the tablet porter would reappear to deliver the northbound tablet to the driver of the Wab train engine up in front, and then continue on to open the points at the north end of the loop to let us out … In a few more seconds, calm and quiet would once again descend on Waianakarua.

V

Shortages of imported coal had, during the Great War, meant NZR having to curtail services. The timing was awful if unavoidable: the system in the 1920s was struggling to reestablish itself just as motor transport was growing and taking much of the railway business. In fact, the annual railway statement delivered in 1925 by the then minister (and future Prime Minister) Gordon Coates is riddled with commentary on the growing challenge both from motor buses and motor lorries. And it also included complaints that the road transport industry made no contribution to the upkeep of roads while NZR had to pay the full cost of maintaining its infrastructure, a complaint that remains familiar today.

But in Coates the NZR had a friend and supporter. The other theme that emerges from his 1925 report tabled in the House of Representatives was the level of activity: reading it today, it sounds almost frenetic and a world away from the present era of reduced railway services (and public profile). The railway board was in 1925 anxious to phase out mixed trains and replace them with railcars to provide speedier non-express services (although it would be many years before they disappeared: even an excursion train from Invercargill to Bluff in 1951, when three large overseas vessels were in port at the same time and an open day was declared, involved the running of the excursion with a mixed train and considerable shunting at intermediate stations, the author and his parents being among the frustrated passengers). In 1925, though, a start had been made on finding better ways to serve passengers on secondary lines: the report noted that the Sentinel steam railcar was doing trial runs on the Melling to Wellington suburban service, and orders had been placed with overseas manufacturers for a Clayton steam railcar and an Edison storage battery car.

The 1925 report also laid out plans to encourage more tourists to use the railway system. The expresses connecting Wellington with New Plymouth and Napier had their journey times reduced to better compete with road transport; similar timetable improvements had been introduced for the Invercargill-Christchurch express and mail trains working from Dunedin to Invercargill and Christchurch. A new sleeping car had been designed, containing nine twin compartments each with running hot and cold water; the department was also looking at introducing an all-sleeper train between Auckland and Wellington (although that would not happen until 1971). A new Auckland-Wellington express had been introduced, along with passenger services from Christchurch to Parnassus in North Canterbury. A fast train now left Ashburton each morning, running to Christchurch and then returning in the later afternoon. The report noted that the introduction of 'ladies' cars' on long-distance expresses had proved very popular.

Expansion was the theme. The railway workshops were being reorganised in 1925 to phase out the small provincial ones and expand those in Auckland, Wellington, Christchurch and Dunedin. New marshalling yards were planned for Wellington and Auckland while many smaller stations were having their yards expanded in order to increase capacity for freight handling. Stockyards had been added at Kauana, a flag station on the Kingston branch in Southland, a loading bank provided at Makarau on the North Auckland line. Several ladies' waiting rooms had been added at smaller stations, including Kaipara Flats (also on the North Auckland line).

In 1925 NZR was operating 662 locomotives, 1,570 passenger carriages, 460 brake vans and 26,028 goods wagons. On order were forty-nine new 4-6-2 Ab steam locomotives for express and freight workings and ten 4-6-4 Ws engines for use on suburban services. The department had placed orders for fifty-five new carriages, eight brake-vans, 108 bogie wagons and 511 four-wheel ones.

In that financial year the rail system consumed 350,000 tons of coal, carried 7,033,459 tons of freight and livestock, laid 189,720 sleepers and spread 155,300 cubic yards of ballast.

Steam

First steam raised: 8 August 1863, by locomotive Lady Barkly on the Southland Provincial Council railway. The first steam working in Canterbury occurred on 16 November 1863, when a locomotive pulled a ballast train on the line between Christchurch and Ferrymead.

Last scheduled steam working on revenue main line operations: 25 October 1971 on Christchurch-Dunedin overnight express.

Steam, in the form of a few remaining still working J and Ja locomotives (the remainder of the NZR network was being operated by diesel-electric traction) lasted only as long as it did — until late 1971 — because the Sunday and Friday night expresses between Dunedin and Christchurch required steam engines to heat the carriages, critical in the cold southern winters. From that date, however, train-heating vans became available for use on the express services and diesel-electric locomotives then hauled all passenger trains.

Even as technology developed, there were limiting factors on the types of steam locomotives that could be designed and built for the New Zealand railway system, primarily the restrictions imposed by the size of the bridges and tunnels designed by the engineers responsible for building the early lines.

There was always noise and movement with a steam locomotive, even if it was only the sound of an engine simmering between roster duties. Here Ka 937 and J 1247 are pictured at the Napier locomotive depot in 1960. (*Bob Stott*)

The longevity of steam engines was illustrated no better than by the example of the Ab class, introduced in 1915 and with class members rolling out of the workshops until 1927; most of these engines survived into the 1960s, with a few remaining on the NZR roster until 1971. As Bob Stott wrote in *Rails* magazine in 1971, 'the class worked in all districts in New Zealand and handled every conceivable task. Abs ran the crack expresses in their earlier days; they were equally at home on goods trains; they ran suburban services, work trains and even shunted in the major marshalling yards'. The 4-6-2 locomotive was designed by NZR, weighed 86.8 tons (engine and tender) and carried 4.5 tons of coal. The first batch of eighteen were built at Addington workshops at Christchurch between 1915 and 1917 with the road number beginning at 608, the first Ab being named Passchendaele after the end of the first war. (Ab 608 was retired by NZR in 1967 and has now been restored to working order by Steam Incorporated.) Addington turned out twenty more Ab locomotives by 1926; then eighty-three more were produced by the North British Locomotive Company in Scotland and twenty were constructed by the North Island engineering company located at Thames, A and G Price. The Ab was the dominant main line locomotive until 1939 when the K and J classes took over the hauling the heavier, faster trains. (Two Ab class engines were chosen in 1971 to be overhauled for use on the Kingston Flyer tourist train ran excursions on the old Kingston branch in Southland; as of 2014, the service was suspended and the two locomotives were in storage at the Kingston station.)

One of the few survivors of the fleet of workhorses that once powered the New Zealand rail system. Ab 795 in 1971 was chosen as one of the two of that class to be retained in service for the Kingston Flyer tourist train that ran on the Kingston branch in Southland. (*Roy Sinclair*)

The end of steam in 1971 had come relatively quickly. Just seventeen years earlier, NZR's fleet of 718 locomotives contained only seventy-one diesel or electric machines. The NZR locomotive fleet as at 31 March 1954, covered a wide variety of types that, today, would horrify cost accountants and fleet managers concerned with efficiency and compatibility. In fact, there were thirty-four classes of steam locomotives, if you count as two those types that were either coal or oil burning. There were 149 Ab engines, making them by far the most numerous. Then followed the Ww tank engines (sixty-four), the A class (fifty-eight) and the oil-burning Ka (thirty-four). Among those at the bottom of the list were the W tank and the Wg tank locomotives (two of each), the Y, We and coal-burning K classes (three of each) and the X, Wb and Q (four each). The fleet also contained the six H class Fell engines used on the Rimutaka Incline. And in 1965 — just six years before steam was phased out and two years before its demise in the North Island — NZR still had 317 steam locomotives on its books, although the writing was on the wall with the fleet also containing 159 main line diesel electrics, forty-six diesel electric shunters, 148 diesel mechanical shunters, twenty-eight electric locomotives and about fifty railcars.

A few locomotives were kept in service after their withdrawal to provide steam. In 1975 it was reported that three K locomotives minus cylinders and cabs were providing steam for the Hutt Workshops, while a stripped engine (it was either a J or Ja) was used for the same purpose at the locomotive depot in Dunedin (its noon whistle being heard over much of the city).

Advertising

After the election of the Labour Government in 1935, many locomotives were painted with the slogan "Buy N.Z-made Goods". The tanks of Wab and tenders of K, A and Ab locomotives carried this message at a time when New Zealand was facing a severe balance of payments problem. Advertising also appeared on wagons at about this time in the South Island, with companies including Timaru Brewery, Bell Tea and Canterbury Frozen Meat using the sides of goods rolling stock to promote their brands. In more modern times Tranz Rail used the sides of modern rolling stock to promote its services, while other wagons carry commercial messages for other products, including soft drinks.

Dining cars

The advent of the Southerner train and its buffet car in 1970 meant the return of a meals service aboard NZR trains for the first time since 1917, although the following year the introduction of the Silver Star saw passengers once again being served at tables in a conventional dining car. The Southerner car was also noteworthy for the fact that, unlike earlier dining cars, it sold alcohol.

The Wellington and Manawatu Railway Company inaugurated dining cars when, in 1887, it coupled its refreshment car to trains between Wellington and Longburn. This car was equipped with a stove, but the absence of end platforms meant passengers could enter and leave the refreshment vehicle only when the train stopped at intermediate stations. Such was its success, however, that the company promptly replaced it with an end-platform car, allowing passengers access while the train was in motion. Several other dining cars were introduced by WMR, including the 1904 car that came from the United States complete with refrigerator, electric lighting, cupboards, stoves and washing-up area. An interesting sidelight is that WMR took on fresh food along the way: bread at Johnsonville, mushrooms and fruit at Paekakariki, peaches, plums and apples at Paraparaumu, fresh trout at Waikanae, vegetables, eggs and poultry at Otaki and more fish at Levin.

The government began looking at dining cars as early as 1895, and in 1899 the construction of four such vehicles was approved. These were built at Addington workshops and entered service between Dunedin and Christchurch on 21 December of that year. Three refreshment cars were made available in 1901 for Wellington-Napier trains and for Wellington-New Plymouth (the latter used in conjunction with WMR services). In 1904 further cars entered service, this time on Auckland-Rotorua trains. The last service to get these cars was the Auckland-Wellington express in 1909. By 1917 NZR had twenty-two dining cars in use.

The NZR operated five 'sittings' depending on the timetable: there was allowance for breakfast, morning tea, luncheon, afternoon tea and tea (the last closing at 7.00 pm). Meals cost two shillings. Passengers at luncheon could choose from fish, hot joints, grills, cold joints, potatoes, salad, cheese, puddings, fruit, tea, coffee or cocoa.

NZR's involvement with dining cars was short-lived. In October 1909, just ten months after absorbing the WMR, the government railway withdrew dining cars from Wellington-Palmerston North trains. In their last years most dining car services were losing money, and in 1917 their total withdrawal coincided with NZR taking over control of refreshment rooms that previously had been leased to private operators: at Mercer, Frankton, Marton, Palmerston North and Hawera in the North Island and, in the South Island, Ashburton and Oamaru. Refreshments were also henceforth provided at Christchurch and Dunedin. After the war ended in 1918, it was decided not to re-introduce the dining cars because of coal and manpower shortages, and haulage power was needed to provide the maximum number of passenger cars on long distance trains.

Refreshment Rooms

Refreshment rooms were scattered throughout the NZR rail network and disappeared only when onboard catering became available and the necessity for long stops (so that steam locomotives could be watered) no longer applied, hastened by the withdrawal of passenger services (most dramatically when railcar operations on secondary lines ceased). There were set-table, sit-down dining rooms at Frankton, Marton, Otira and Oamaru (and, in early days, also at Woodville and Clinton). But most

NZR refreshment rooms were counter service operations, offering pies, sandwiches, cakes, tea and soft drinks. There were also at one time fifteen privately leased stalls at minor stations such as Te Karaka on the Gisborne section (later Moutohora branch) and at Tadmor on the Nelson line. Private operations appeared at many smaller stations in early years.

On the North Island Main Trunk passenger services entailed refeshment stops at Paekakariki, Palmerston North, Marton, Taihape, Tuamarunui, Te Kuiti, Frankton Junction and Mercer. The last mentioned station was used by most Main Trunk services as a refreshment stop and also for passengers travelling on the Taneatua Express trains. The New Zealand poet A. R. D. Fairburn is said to have once declaimed: 'The squalid tea of Mercer is not strained'.

A trip southwards on the South Island express services in the 1950s afforded the opportunity to get off the train for food and drinks at Ashburton, Timaru, Oamaru (where there was a full sit-down dining room for lunch, the train stopping for twenty-four minutes to allow passengers to consume three courses), Palmerston, Dunedin, Milton and Clinton (the Gore refreshment rooms also opened for northbound trains). Train travellers were accustomed to seeing the floors of carriages littered with clinking empty teacups, plates and soft drink bottles, until the porter came through and collected the crockery and bottles.

* * *

Taihape railway station about 1915 with the refreshment room in the foreground, the building hosting many advertisements including ones for Amber Tips tea (a popular New Zealand brand), Winfred cigarettes, a local bakery, a furnishing company in Wanganui and Van Houten's cocoa. (*Photograph by F. G. Radcliff, now held by Alexander Turnbull Library, Wellington*)

The refreshment room at Taihape in 1988 — more utilitarian than elegant. (*Bob Stott*)

In 1932, *New Zealand Railways Magazine* listed all the then open refreshment rooms. Going north from Auckland, passengers could buy food and drink at Helensville, Maungaturoto and Whangarei; on the North Island Main Trunk there were refreshment rooms at Auckland, Mercer, Frankton Junction, Taumarunui, Ohakune, Taihape, Marton, Palmerston North,and Paekakariki; in the Bay of Plenty rooms existed at Paeroa, Tauranga and Putaruru; travelling to New Plymouth allowed for refreshments at Aramoho, Patea and Hawera; on the Hawke's Bay line in 1932 just at Woodville and Waipukurau; on the Wairarapa line, Kaitoke and Masterton had refreshment rooms. In the South Island in 1932, they operated at Christchurch, Otira, Ashburton, Oamaru, Palmerston, Dunedin, Clinton and Gore. In 1932, the Minister of Railways reported that, due to the Great Depression, sales had dropped significantly (NZR would drop prices soon after this) and in the year to March the refreshments branch had dispensed 1.23 million cups of tea, coffee or cocoa, 1.11 million sandwiches and pies and 115,660 set meals. In 1933 Wellington's Evening Post reported complaints about NZR refreshment services, including the fact that a cup of tea and two sandwiches cost one shilling, a sum which elsewhere would have purchased a full dinner, while at one unnamed station in the North Island cattle trucks were parked on a siding opposite the rooms, leading to an infestation of flies in the refreshment room while people ate.

Christchurch had a large dining room, which was thronged after the arrival of the boat train from Lyttelton with travellers having a solid breakfast before the departure of the southern express. Wellington, too, possessed a very large dining room, which was extremely busy in the mornings, especially with hungry and often bleary-eyed travellers alighting from the Main Trunk expresses from Auckland or having walked from the nearby interisland ferry wharf after travelling overnight by sea from Lyttelton.

The food through the refreshment room service was plain but wholesome in the style New Zealanders of the time expected. For example, at the dining rooms at Frankton in the late 1930s you could have a four-course meal, starting with soup, followed by an entree, then the choice of hot or cold meats with lettuce or cooked vegetables, followed by a choice of puddings including plum pudding and jelly. Then followed tea, coffee or cocoa with biscuits and cheese.

At Ohakune on the North Island Main Trunk (and junction for the Raetihi branch line) the refreshment rooms were open all day and most of the night, not only serving passenger trains but as a meeting place by local people. The rooms were popular with the people who travelled into Ohakune on Saturday evenings to attend the town's cinema on what were called the 'picture trains' from Waiouru and National Park. One member of staff employed there during the First World War recalled the busy nights: the northbound Wellington to Auckland express arrived at 9.10 pm and the southbound one at 4.20 am; in between there were troops trains full of hungry soldiers wanting food and tea.

An unusual arrangement existed at Ranfurly on the Otago Central line. Trains (and, later, railcars) stopped there for refreshments, but passengers were required to leave the station and go to either the town's hotel or private tea rooms.

Fire was a problem. In 1985, flames broke out in the privately-run refreshment room at Te Aute in Hawke's Bay, destroying the station. (Napier's Daily Telegraph reported the suspect was a boy who had been arrested at Waipara for stealing whisky and was being transported on the express by police). In 1900 the Clinton refreshment room caught ablaze taking the station and post office with it. A year earlier, the owner of the refreshment operation at Aramoho near Wanganui, Mrs Jubal Fleming, was out of pocket to the tune £100 (after insurance) when her rooms were burnt down. Other rooms to suffer a similar fate were Marton (1921), Moana on the West Coast (1926) and Lumsden in Southland in 1935.

Crockery items on the NZR system were numbered according to which refreshment rooms they belonged. There was also colour coding in the South Island in the early years of the twentieth century. If a passenger was drinking tea from a cup with green markings, that item belonged to the rooms at Otira. Brown meant Christchurch, blue Ashburton, red Oamaru, orange Palmerston, and grey came from Dunedin. Gore's crockery bore the words "Govt Rlys" encircled in blue. In later years individual 'ownership' of crockery was abolished and plain 'NZR' marking was adopted.

In the early days, liquor was served at most of the privately leased refreshment rooms. But this was gradually eliminated in the early years of the twentieth century.

But, just as it had in the years before the First World War, NZR found its post-1971 reintroduction of on-board catering an expensive proposition. The department was spending $8 million a year but earning just $4.3 million and soon came to the conclusion that the food being offered was too elaborate; meals disappeared from the Northerner (Auckland–Wellington) and Southerner (Christchurch–Invercargill) and were replaced with sandwiches, cakes and hot savouries. The Endeavour (on the Wellington–Napier run) lost its buffet car altogether, NZR deciding it was not justified on a five and a half hour journey.

2
Trains for all Occasions

NEW ZEALAND'S APPROACH TO passenger services in the latter part of the twentieth century had often been of the 'make do and mend' variety. The Ac passenger cars were probably the best illustration of this. When the Fiat-powered 88-seat railcars were ending the end of their life in the late 1970s, it was decided to convert fourteen of them into passenger carriages, with their engines and driver cabins removed. They were generally known as 'grassgrubs' due to their green and grey colour scheme. The carriages ran on locomotive-hauled trains on various secondary lines (Napier to Gisborne, the Wairarapa and Okahukura lines, for example) but they did not last long, the last four two-carriage sets in operation being withdrawn in April 1985.

In 1991 the Silver Fern railcars were withdrawn from North Island Main Trunk services, NZR invented the Geyserland Express (Auckland-Rotorua) and Kaimai Express (Auckland-Tauranga) as a means of both finding a new use for the railcars and also as a trial to reestablish passenger runs on secondary lines.

With the first upgraded long-distance trains introduced in the 1970s, the Southerner and Endeavour, these used reconditioned steel carriages built between 1937 and 1945. Auckland suburban services were maintained by importing diesel-multiple units that had been superseded on the Perth, Australia, system (that also operates on the 1,067 mm gauge) while British Rail Mark II coaches were imported longer distance services and re-gauged from their original 1,435 mm wheels.

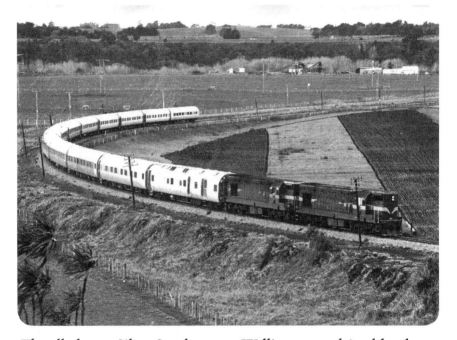

The all-sleeper Silver Star between Wellington and Auckland was certainly one of the great travelling experiences on New Zealand Railways — for the comparatively short time it lasted. The train offered good food and comfortable beds, a long way from hard seats in the second-class carriages, pies and tea served in thick cups on offer at various stations, and pillows on the overnight expresses in the steam era. Here two Da class locomotives round a bend near Marton in 1971. (*NZR — Bob Stott collection*)

But some trains were brand new — the prime examples being the all-sleeper Silver Star train sets and the Silver Fern railcars, all built in Japan for the Auckland-Wellington service. And there were earlier examples, including the Rotorua Limited.

Rotorua Limited

Introduced: 5 May 1930

Name changed: To Rotorua Express, 1934

Withdrawn: 1958. Replaced by 88-seater Fiat-powered diesel railcars.

This service from Auckland was conceived as a means by which tourists would travel to the resorts at Rotorua, the city famous for its geothermal attractions (from mineral baths to bubbling mud pools to geysers). In its first few years the train included an observation car which was described as having Oriental carpet, silver fittings and blue silk curtains; however, this car was withdrawn as an economy measure during the Great Depression and converted into a second-class passenger carriage. The inaugural service consisted of two first-class carriages, four second-class cars, the observation car, and a guard's van.

The cover on one of the early editions of Rails magazine (found-ed in 1971 by Bob Stott and Robin Bromby) purported to show the interior of the observation car on the Rotorua Limited, a train inaugurated in 1930. But the photo was probably taken in 1929 inside the lounge car introduced that year on the Daylight Express, the train operating between Wellington and Auckland. But the picture certainly captures one of the occasional attempts by NZR to provide more comfort on long distance trains, both the Daylight Express and Rotorua Limited efforts undone by the approaching Great Depression.

In its latter years, and by now known as the Rotorua Express, patronage kept falling as the department's bus services were more popular as a means of getting to Rotorua; in 1954 the train was running only on Mondays and Fridays, although the Christmas-New Year period saw it back to six days a week.

On 2 June 1930, *New Zealand Railways Magazine* featured an article by London-based journalist J.C. Morrison on the Rotorua Limited:

'There was a large crowd of people on the platform at the Auckland station as the new express steamed out punctually. (A replica of the Auckland express left Rotorua at the same hour, 10.10 am, for Auckland). Our express was composed of two first-class carriages, four second-class carriages, an observation car, a guard's van, and a powerful locomotive. The train was full to capacity.

'As our express gradually slackened its rate of speed and came to a standstill at Frankton Junction, we were afforded a most excellent close-up view of our twin-sister express, which had just arrived from Rotorua. Those of us who had seen Stevenson's original "Puffing Billy" and "carriages", now on exhibition in the South Kensington Museum, in London, made a mental comparison of these relics of the railway inception period, with the artistic beauty and luxuriousness of the new expresses.

'(At) Frankton Junction, we found the station packed with enthusiastic sightseers. Most of them were sturdy farmers and their families, who "scorn delights and live laborious days" on dairy farms nearby.

'They gazed in open-eyed wonderment at the splendour of the new expresses, with the richly emblazoned coat of arms on the outside of each carriage. This conspicuous adornment drew the attention of those who had seen the official Ministerial coaches with the royal arms painted in colours. Although these new coaches resemble the official cars in appearance, with respect to new contrivances the former are really more artistically finished and far more up-to-date.

'After leaving Frankton, passengers went from end to end of the train examining everything, particularly the observation car with its beautiful Oriental carpet, its exquisite oxidised silver fittings, and dainty blue silk curtains hanging on its wide, low, plate-glass windows. These latter fit into felt guides, and are balanced with a leather spring arrangement, making for easy operation and eliminating any possibility of the windows rattling against their frames. The electric lighting, ventilation, and heating arrangements, also were greatly admired. The light, softly diffused through cut glass globes, is pleasing and restful to the eye. At the back of each of the richly upholstered reversible armchairs is a tiny electric reading light. In addition to electric fans and ceiling ventilation, glass slides, moving easily between felt guides, are provided over the windows for ventilation purposes.

'We note that the whole train is connected by concertina vestibules, both dust-proof and wind-proof. This innovation will be very much appreciated by the travelling public. These twin Auckland-Rotorua expresses are the only trains of the kind on the New Zealand Railways. By the passengers, one heard perhaps more praise lavished on the corridors than any other part of the train — and that is saying a great deal.

'The first-class carriages are designed to give travellers 'ample room and comfort. The very latest style in armchairs is provided, these being furnished in rich blue moquette, of very serviceable texture, making a striking contrast with the silver-plated seating frames. The chairs can be easily adjusted to three different positions. The interior decorations are all of choice and beautifully polished New Zealand timbers.

'One heard the remark passed that it would be almost desecration to cover these artistic furnishings with advertisements, as is done on other trains. The windows (with the exception of width), the heating and ventilation, and the electric lights (excepting the small reading lamps) are much the same as those installed in .the observation car.

'In each first-class carriage is a birdcage compartment to seat six persons. These may be reserved for persons desiring privacy while travelling. Except with regard to the seating accommodation, there is no difference in the design of the second-class carriages. The armchairs are covered with imitation leather of pleasing tone, but there is slightly less cushioned ease in the upholstery than in that of the first-class seats. However, the comfort facilities provided are a wonderful improvement on those of other cars. The exteriors of all the carriages are finished in Vitron enamel panels of Midland Lake Red.

'To ensure smooth running, all springs used are specially tempered, and the bogies of longer wheel-base than in use on other carriages. To minimise side shocks, which are experienced when rounding curves or travelling over crossings, these bogies are also fitted with bolster buffers. By an ingenious contrivance the water supply is controlled from underneath each carriage, where it is contained in tanks of high capacity. Raised by mean of air pressure of from seven to ten pounds per square inch, it passes through a heater governed by steam from the locomotive. Thus a supply of hot water, sufficient for the lavatory basin throughout the trip, is maintained.

'Another interesting contrivance is an easily operated emergency brake, connected with the Westinghouse brake and fitted inside each carriage. One other feature is the new automatic couplings, manipulated by a lever, from the side of the carriage. These are designed 'to ensure absolute safety, not only to passengers, but also to shunters whenever the latter are called upon to detach cars.

'These are the most striking features of the new "Wonder Trains". Although I have copious notes about places of interest passed on the way to Rotorua, I find that I have used all the space allotted me in describing (very imperfectly perhaps) the splendid arrangements of these new expresses, and must, therefore eliminate all reference to the prosperous butter factories and the amazingly successful development of the country passed through (en route to Rotorua). Our express reached its destination at scheduled time, its arrival being enthusiastically greeted by a large crowd, whose interest and pride in the magnificent train was manifest on all sides.'

[This article first published in *Rails* magazine, January 1972]

Excursion Trains

Excursion trains were popular in many areas of the country in the years before motorcar ownership became widespread. As soon as railway lines were laid, it seems, there were plans for excursion trains — remembering that, for the early decades of the system, it was otherwise impractical for city dwellers to move far beyond their towns other than by train. In 1876, for example, an excursion train is recorded as travelling from Oamaru to Moeraki to give townsfolk the opportunity to visit the huge boulders that dot the beach there. It was common, too, for excursion trains to be run along a newly opened section of line or for celebrations marking the completion of a new branch.

Excursion trains were particularly popular with the people of Invercargill, and there is a record of one picnic train in the late 1870s consisting of fifteen carriages. On the Prince of Wales' birthday on 9 November 1879, Invercargill station sold 479 tickets for an excursion train to Bluff (complete with a brass band for entertainment), fifty-five tickets for people on an outing to Winton and sixty-two for those setting out to Mataura for the day.

Picnic trains ran on many lines, some organised by employers for staff outings, For example, Kaiapoi Woollen Mills near Christchurch each year sent its staff on a picnic outing by rail. In the earlier deacdes of rail, most provincial centres had passenger carriages based locally, so organising excursion trains was not a great challenge. Excursion trains ran from Stratford to allow residents of that town a day by the sea at New Plymouth; Caroline Bay at Timaru was another popular seaside excursion destination. In November 1927 four hundred excursionists were transported from Wellington to Wanganui, NZR arranging for concession rates with the owners of private river vessels that took sightseers up the Wanganui River to visit a Maori village, with lunch and afternoon tea served on the boat. The cost, including rail fare, boat trip and food, was £1.11s 8d first class, £1.4s 4d second class.

Then there were the Daffodil trains that took excursionists to Lawrence on the Roxburgh branch, mainly from Dunedin but also from Invercargill, to view the hillsides that each year were covered by the flowers. Children's outings were also common, such as the annual train laid on for the young of Ormondville in Hawke's Bay for a day visit to Napier. Early Royal tours also required special excursion trains to take people to see the visitors; in 1920, for example, NZR ran a special from Lawrence on the Roxburgh branch to Milton so that schoolchildren could cheer the Prince of Wales when he passed through the latter town by train.

Back in the days when provincial centres had access to a mixture of passenger rolling stock, NZR was able to organise excursion trains. In 1960 a special for Napier Shopping Week nears the end of its morning journey from the provincial town of Waipukurau. (*Bob Stott*)

At the beginning of the 1900s, Thos. Cook and Son offered a number of excursion packages, some combined with sea journeys. Aucklanders could take the train to connect with a steamer at Helensville travelling to Thames; upon landing at the latter, they would travel by train to Te Aroha and then on to Rotorua. The travel agency promoted outings to Waingaro Hot Springs involving train travel as far as Ngaruawahia; similarly, tourists could visit Waitomo Caves after leaving the train at Otorohanga. Or there were trips to Cambridge for its inland climate.

In the South Island, Thos. Cook could arrange a package which involved travelling by steamer across Cook Strait from Wellington to Picton, continuing by train as far as Blenheim, then by coach to Nelson, back on the NZR system from Nelson to the then end of the rails at Motupiko, another coach trip to Reefton, rail to Hokitika, and finally by coach again to Franz Joseph Glacier.

Even as late as the early 1950s NZR was still catering for special outings, one regular outing being trains running from Wellington to Hastings for the annual Blossom Festival in the Hawke's Bay centre. In the 1970s, before the private Taieri Gorge operation was contemplated, NZR operated trains during Festival Week to Pukerangi on the Otago Central line. Excursion trains still run from Wellington to Featherston for New Year's race meetings and for a popular wine festival at Martinborough in the Wairarapa.

Broadcasting Train

In 1939 the National Commercial Broadcasting Service, as the commercial state-owned radio stations were then known, was looking to expand commercial radio beyond the main cities. It was therefore decided to convert a railway carriage into a broadcasting studio, complete with a three-man crew, a retractable antenna and low-power transmitter. The station was given the call sign of 5ZB, and the intention was to gauge the audience — and advertising — potential in various provincial towns of the North Island. The station first went on the air in Rotorua in April 1939, and in seventy-nine days covered 2,650 km of the NZR system. Station 5ZB entertained radio audiences in Hamilton, Whangarei, Te Kuiti, Taumarunui, New Plymouth, Hawera, Wanganui, Palmerston North, Dannevirke, Napier, Hastings and Masterton. More than 15,000 curious listeners inspected the mobile station during its travels. The 5ZB manager wanted to keep the station going, his plan being to have the carriage do three month-long stints in various locations. His masters, however, decided instead to gradually open permanent stations in various towns. Both plans were shelved due to the war.

In 1982 the Pleasant Point Railway and Historical Society refitted guard's van F423 with vintage radio equipment, and some broadcasts were made from this rail studio via the local Timaru station, 3ZC.

Coal Trains

While coal is now carried over the New Zealand railway system mainly for export, it once constituted an important domestic freight component in the days when householders and industries used coal for heating and steam. Then, of course, NZR was also required to transport considerable quantities for use in its national steam locomotive fleet.

It was coal that laid the economic basis for the rail system on the South Island's west coast. So the first line, between Greymouth and Brunnerton, was built to haul coal from the Brunner and other mines in that locality to the wharf in Greymouth. Rail also made possible the extraction of coal from mines which would have been inaccessible in any practicable way by road at the time — thus the Blackball and Rewanui branches, with their incline sections, enabled the Roa and Liverpool mines to be exploited. The Denniston Incline, connecting with the short Conn's Creek branch, was the most spectacular example of how rail opened up the coal industry.

Coal dominated the operations of the ports at Greymouth and Westport. In 1910 about 700,000 tons of coal was railed into Westport for shipment. Greymouth's wharves that same year handled just under 400,000 tons — again, most of it brought to the ships in rail wagons. At the Westport coal stathes, wagons were run up an inclined road to the top of the structure, where the wagon bottom doors were opened to allow the coal to fall between the rails into hoppers under the decking. Shutes from the bottoms of these hoppers were lowered to allow coal to be dropped into the ships' holds. Further along the wharf, steam cranes lifted the removable hoppers from Q class wagons and swung them over a ship's hatches. At Greymouth the line ran on to the railway wharf where wagons had their coal unloaded into shoots for transferring into a ship's hold. The opening of the Otira tunnel in 1923, along with the reduction in dependence on coal as the main source of the nation's energy, saw the start of the decline for these two ports, a situation worsened by the Great Depression, and in fiscal 1933 coal railed to Westport wharves totalled just 282,163 tons.

Railways played an important part in transporting coal when the colliers arrived at ports in other parts of New Zealand. NZR in the early years of the twentieth century kept a fleet of R and Rb wagons at Wellington railway wharf where colliers unloaded; in Dunedin sidings ran into coal merchants' yards located near the station. As late as 1953 the NZR annual report showed that 'products of mines' (almost all coal) provided 24.83 per cent of goods revenues. Nevertheless, the trend was obvious: coal haulage in 1953 was 155,073 tons lower than in 1952.

Several lines in the North Island owed their existence to coal traffic. Kawakawa was linked to Opua in 1868 to allow for shipment of coal (this being the North Island's earliest railway), and the first rails out of Whangarei went to Kamo where coal mining was under way. The line from Frankton to Thames was originally laid to allow the transport of coal to the goldfields. From Huntly, the nearby coalfields were opened up by the completion in 1924 of the Glen Afton branch. Coal was also an important traffic for some years on the Stratford-Okahukura line; the Egmont Coal Company operated a tramway to meet the NZR system at Tangarakau station. In the South Island the Wairio (Southland) and Whitecliffs (Canterbury) branches owed their existence to coal traffic. Coal was an early mainstay of traffic on the Browns branch in Southland.

Today the continued operation of the Midland line depended on the coal traffic from the West Coast to Lyttelton.

Grain Trains

While the building of railways across Canterbury during and after the Vogel construction boom helped develop the grain industry by providing economic transport for farmers, it was grain in turn that sustained the railway system throughout the province. From Waikari on the Waiau line to Studholme Junction on the South Island's main trunk line, westwards to Sheffield on the Midland line and on the Southbridge branch (which was built primarily to carry wheat from farms south of Christchurch), grain traffic keep station staff and sidings busy in the harvest season. The traffic also played a big part in the economics of several other Canterbury branch lines. According to the *New Zealand Historical Atlas*, the railway figures for 1890 show that 5,964 tons of grain were consigned from Pleasant Point on the Fairlie branch that year, 20,351 tons from Rakaia and 5,433 tons from Lincoln Junction, the meeting of the Southbridge and Little River branches. On what is now the Main South line, important grain shipment stations in 1890 included Hornby Junction, Rolleston, Dunsandel, Chertsey, Ashburton, Hinds, Rangitata, Winchester, Temuka, St Andrews and Makikihi. Big shipments on the line north of Christchurch came from Kaiapoi, Amberley, Styx, Sefton, Rangiora and Belfast; on the Midland line, Kirwee and Darfield were busy wheat shipment centres. On branch lines, the atlas also identifies Fairlie and Albury (Fairlie branch), Southbridge, Doyleston and Ellesmere (Southbridge branch) and Oxford West, Bennetts Junction and Cust (Oxford branch) as significant wheat consignment stations.

Limiteds

The last NZR designated 'Limited' train ran on 4 September 1971, with the Silver Star service from the following day replacing the old Auckland-Wellington Limiteds. The last South Island Limited had disappeared the previous December when the Southerner started on the Christchurch-Invercargill route. While the term had originated in the United States as a system whereby passengers were partially refunded for late running, the use of 'Limited' in New Zealand usually applied to trains with fewer stops than other expresses. Thus, the South Island Limited referred to the express service introduced between Christchurch and Invercargill on 1 August 1949, which saw a reduction in the journey time between the two cities by one hour and six minutes to 11 hr 20 min. The service initially operated on Monday, Wednesday and Friday of each week, stopping at Ashburton, Timaru, Oamaru, Palmerston, Dunedin, Milton, Balclutha, Clinton and Gore. The 'Limited' was followed by another passenger train, which served many smaller stations along the route. On Tuesdays, Thursdays and Saturdays only one train ran either way, this express service including ten stops not on the 'Limited' timetable, such as Rakaia, Temuka, Edendale and Woodlands. Like other expresses of this era, the Limited consisted of both first and second-class cars. Subsequently, in 1956, the Invercargill-Christchutch Limited effectively lost much of its status when it was required to stop at twenty-one stations.

Log Trains

The long logging train hauled by powerful diesel locomotives is a relatively recent development on the New Zealand rail system. But cut timber was an important source of business for most of NZR's existence. Several lines were built to gain access to native timber: the Raetihi and Catlins River branches were just two among many. Once the line from Napier southwards to the Hawke's Bay hinterland was built, for example, timber from the interior provided much of its early revenue (and railway sleepers). Woodville, Dannevirke, Makotuku, Ormondville, Takapau, Waipawa and Te Aute were all important stations for timber consignment. Many other stations — mainly in the North Island — were important timber centres where bush tramways fed their loads on to NZR trains: Ongarue, Manunui and Pokaka were some examples on the North Island Main Trunk, Mamaku and Selwyns on the Rotorua branch. In the Bay of Plenty the Whakatane Board Mills ran its own railway in the form of the Matahina tramway and another line from the East

Coast Main Trunk to its mill in Whakatane. Almost every station between Otira and Greymouth on the Midland line had a bush tramway running off into the hills or forest.

Logging traffic has been one of the main growth sectors for New Zealand's railway system since the Second World War. While branch lines were being closed throughout the country in the 1950s and 1960s, 101 km of branch lines (to Kinleith and Murupara) were constructed to tap new forest resources. There have also been proposals to build other lines (to Taupo, for example) or re-lay closed lines (Moutohora) to carry logs. In 2000 the Dargaville branch in Northland was re-opened on the basis of the amount of log traffic available for rail transport.

Mail on Trains

Mail was first carried on a New Zealand train by the Southland Provincial government (to Makarewa from Invercargill) on 27 April 1865. In October 1878, on the government system, the first Railway Travelling Post Office (RTPO) operated between Christchurch and Dunedin, a service that was extended to Invercargill in January 1879. (The vans were removed from the Invercargill section in 1931 and withdrawn from Christchurch-Dunedin in 1942.) By 1881 NZR was providing mail transport on fifty trains operating around the country. A parcel post service was offered from 1887.

There were RTPOs on the Wellington-New Plymouth route between 1886 and 1931, and between Auckland and Thames between 1903 and 1928, with the service operating from Auckland to Paeroa for another three years. The mail cars were introduced between Auckland and Hamilton in 1901 and later expanded to the North Island Main Trunk and to Napier. Trains that hauled these vans soon became known for that function, being referred to, for example, as the Napier Mail or the 'Down Mail' to New Plymouth. Then there was the Christchurch Mail, a thrice-weekly (and daily, during holiday periods) passenger service operating between Greymouth and Christchurch in the period 1923-1956. The last RTPO was withdrawn in 1971 when the Silver Star superseded the Limited expresses on the North Island Main Trunk.

Until the 1960s virtually all passenger trains (latterly the railcars) carried mail, as did many ordinary goods trains. Canvas mailbags and wickerwork hampers for fragile items were all part of the railway scene, and many of the larger railway stations had space set aside for Post Office workers.

Milk Trains

The first movement of bulk milk by train took place in 1997 from Oringi, south of Dannevirke, to the Kiwi Co-operative Dairies Ltd plant at Whareroa, just south of Hawera. Milk trains also began running from the company's Longburn dairy factory near Palmerston North. By 1999 the New Zealand rail network had a fleet of 66 bulk milk wagons, each capable of holding 52,000 litres.

Milk trains began running on the North Auckland line and, in 1999 bulk milk movements started on the Main South line from a dairy factory at Edendale to Temuka, located near what was then New Zealand's largest dairy processing plant. The traffic in the 2000-2001 season comprised cream and whey protein concentrates from the Edendale factory to Temuka at the rate of 120,000 litres a day. There was also some surplus milk sent by rail from Hokitika on the South Island's west coast to the factory near Temuka, with daily shipments being supplemented by special trains at the weekends.

Mixed Trains

The last scheduled mixed train to operate on NZR rails ran between Whangarei and Opua on 6 June 1977.

Once the backbone of the New Zealand railway passenger system, the ubiquitous mixed train, with its rake of assorted wagons and one or two carriages (often listed as 'goods with car' in timetables), was a part of most railway lines in the country. This was certainly the case until the 1930s when a number of branches lost their passenger services and therefore their mixed trains, but these slow moving, frequently stopping and shunting trains lasted well beyond that decade on many other lines. The 1926 timetable shows on the Morrinsville-Thames section that there were four daily mixed services, one leaving Paeroa, the others from Morrinsville running through to Thames. On the Waihao Downs branch in South Canterbury during the 1920s, all ten trains on weekdays (five in each direction) were mixed, although all but two went only so far as Waimate.

Goods with car attached. Timetables for many lines through-out New Zealand once offered this transport option. On the rural branch lines, such as the Methven branch seen here, the mixed trains were the only form of rail transport that was economically justifiable to the rail operator; on the main lines, these trains provided transport in addition to express trains, such as overnight travel between Christchurch and Dunedin. (*NZR - Bob Stott collection*)

The mixed trains made use of a wide variety of passenger cars. On the Eyreton and Oxford branches, for example, the daily mixed could include an old four-compartment car (first and second classes, each with a smoking and non-smoking compartment).

And it was not just branches that carried mixed trains. In the 1930s, for example, mixed trains ran between Christchurch and Springfield on the Midland line, and well into the 1950s it was possible to travel overnight between Christchurch and Dunedin on the "goods with car", a long and usually sleep-deprived journey due to the frequent stopping and shunting (to which fact the author can attest having been aboard such a Dunedin-bound service in 1955).

In the postwar years the North Island Main Trunk had a series of mixed trains providing daytime services, while the expresses ran along that route at night. In 1972 the goods trains travelling between Wairoa and Gisborne still included an old wooden passenger car each Friday. This was attached in the morning to the Palmerston North-Gisborne freight when it pulled into Wairoa and was then brought back to Wairoa in the afternoon, where it was detached from the train and presumably sat on a siding until the following Friday. Many other mixed trains survived well after the Second World War, including the morning mixed from Rotorua to Frankton, as well as those operating between Greymouth and Hokitika, Taumarunui and Stratford and even on branch lines such as Raetihi. In fact, the Okahukura-Stratford line was one of the last strongholds of the mixed train, with these included in the timetable until the early 1970s.

The latter days of the mixed train. In the far north of the North Island on the Okaihau branch on 8 October 1973, train No. 1040 had just passed the dilapidated station of Lake Omapere Road Crossing behind Da 1512 and was heading into typical scrub country. As photographer Wilson Lythgoe notes: "It's a grubby looking loco so typical of the period when cleaning rags weren't allowed to get anywhere near a loco! It's a reasonable sized train for a branch but the consist could mainly be empty wagons". The carriage at the rear was looking just as dilapidated as the station building. Da 1512 was built by General Motors Canada and had entered service in July/August 1967. (*Wilson Lythgoe*)

Race Trains

In the days before motorcar ownership became widespread and generally affordable, trains were a popular means of travel for a day out at the races. Typical was the situation in 1873 when the races at Ellerslie over the Christmas–New Year period saw what would today be called a 'shuttle' service run by trains between Auckland and the racecourse beginning at 9.00 am; a return service to the course also ran from Onehunga. Two private lines were built primarily to serve race traffic: the Hutt Park Railway Company operation in Wellington and the Dunedin, Peninsula & Ocean Beach Railway to the Forbury Park course.

NZR frequently put on special race trains over much of its network in the era before most people had their own motorcars. On Labour Day, 23 October 1944, the finish of the day's racing at the Oamaru Trotting Club saw two trains depart from the small Racecourse station nearby, one for Timaru at 5.34 pm and one for Oamaru at 5.35 pm. Another working, from Oamaru to the Kurow branch, picked up passengers at the racecourse stop. The race book also shows a special train leaving for Palmerston at 6.00 pm. In addition, there were buses to Ngapara and Tokarahi, passenger services on those branches having been withdrawn in 1926. Another undated page from an Oamaru Trotting Club race book showed the following services:

To Course

From Oamaru: Depart 11.03 am and 11.40 am. (Fare 1s 1d return)
From Dunedin: Depart 7.45 am and 8. 27 am.
From Timaru: Departs 8. 50 am (connects with Waimate branch service)
From Christchurch: Depart 7.07 am, stopping at Ashburton, Temuka and Timaru.

NZR also provided horse transport. At the end of the Oamaru race meeting, a horse train left Racecourse station at 7.15 pm for Timaru and Washdyke, with some horseboxes being detached at Studholme Juntion to be coupled to a Waimate branch train.

The Manawatu Racing Club at Palmerston North was unusual in that it owned its own private siding at Awapuni Racecourse. Race trains took three minutes to run down the private line, which was in service from 24 December 1904 until 31 October 1939. In the same category was Christchurch's Canterbury Jockey Club; as early as 1874, the club began to investigate a siding from Sockburn station to its course nearby. This siding was formally opened on 3 November 1877. Initially, the trains operated non-stop to and from Christchurch and the popularity of the services forced the club to extend the length of the platform at the course. Trains consisted of both carriages and open wagons with seating. A photograph taken in 1949 shows the siding divided into four roads within the club's property. In 1915 the club built a water tank so that NZR could dispense with hauling water wagons to the course for filling locomotives. (By the early years of the twentieth century the Christchurch Tramway Board ran trams to Riccarton racecourse, and there was a tram shed erected on the Jockey Club's land.) The last race trains ran on 10 November 1954 and, after NZR declined to buy the line, the track was lifted.

Race trains were familiar to many Wellingtonians, and these lasted well into the modern era. Trentham station was equipped with a special platform serving the Wellington Racing Club's course. While many people travelled to the races there on scheduled suburban workings, race specials ran from Wellington, terminating at the second platform.

Only one racecourse service survives. On the three days a year the Wairarapa Racing Club holds a meeting at the Tauherinikau in the Wairarapa and trains are run from Wellington through the Rimutaka tunnel to Featherston, the closest station to the racecourse and from which buses complete the journey to the course.

Railcars

New Zealand Railways experimented with a variety of railcar types in order to find a vehicle that was both light and self-contained, as well as being able to achieve economic loads in terms of passenger numbers. But nothing really worked well until NZR came up with the Wairarapa railcars, which entered service in 1936, followed by the reliable and sturdy Standard design.

The first true railcar was the McEwan–Pratt petrol-engined car of 1912, built in Christchurch but considered a complete failure. Then came the Westinghouse petrol-electric car, which entered service in 1914. This railcar was powered from a six-cylinder petrol engine coupled to a 90 horsepower generator that supplied power to two 60 hp traction motors, mounted one to each bogie. It was able to seat forty-eight passengers, and NZR intended that it should also haul a carriage. But the car had insufficient power for this latter task, the defect which telling against the railcar when it was assigned (even without a carriage) to the steeply graded Johnsonville section of what was then the North Island Main Trunk out of Wellington. Another petrol-electric car was introduced in 1916 but saw little service before being scrapped.

In an attempt to find an economic means of transporting passengers on branch lines in the sparsely populated areas, NZR in 1926 introduced two railcars (Rm 4 and Rm 5) based on the one-ton Model T Ford truck chassis. They measured 3.3 metres in length and could carry eleven passengers in addition to the driver. The two railcars were used in Southland, on the Waikaia (then Switzers) and Wyndham (then Glenham) lines, providing connecting services to Riversdale and Edendale respectively, until withdrawn in 1931. But they were uncomfortable to ride in and their lightweight condition led to several derailments. One (Rm 4) has been recreated at the Pleasant Point Museum and Railway and has also been operated on the remnant of line between Kingston and Fairlight used by the Kingston Flyer.

As the website of the Pleasant Point railway museum near Timaru explains, in 1925 New Zealand Railways decided to build two lightweight railcars, placed on a one-ton Model T Ford truck chassis, in Wellington's railway workshops. Their construction was part of a national drive by railways to reduce the costs of operating on light traffic lines where there were only a limited number of passengers. The machines were assigned to Southland; as the website notes, 'rumour has it they were deliberately sent as far away from Wellington as possible' (once it was realised the cars were not comfortable for passengers). The museum has created a replica of Rm 4, and it is seen here at the Keanes Crossing platform at the end of the museum line on 18 July 2013. (*Bryan Blanchard*)

CLAYTON STEAM RAIL CAR FOR PASSENGER SERVICE ARRIVES AT KUROW.
D. H. Gilmour, photo.

The Kurow line in the South Island was one of the few branches that saw railcar services. In 1926 the Clayton steam car was assigned to run up this line from Oamaru, but it was plagued by mechanical problems and was withdrawn in 1928. But the local pride in having a railcar service was evident from this picture taken near Kurow. (*Bob Stott collection*)

Other trials followed: the Buckhurst petrol car in 1926, an Edison storage-battery car which ran for a few years on the Little River branch until it was lost in a depot fire, and two steam-powered railcars, the Sentinel-Cammell car which was used for a short time on the Frankton Junction-Thames line;

51

and the Clayton steam car which was used on the Kurow branch and between Invercargill and Bluff before being dismantled in the Invercargill yards. The Clayton car was imported from the United Kingdom and erected at the Petone workshops. After many (and often troubled-plagued-trial runs in the North Island) the railcar was assigned first to the Kurow branch, where it ran a morning service from that terminus to Oamaru, returning in the afternoon. After being withdrawn in 1928, the car re-appeared on services between Bluff and Invercargill. From 1930 the Clayton was used only intermittently before being withdrawn completely in 1937. Apart from the many problems with the boiler and the fact that it could not tackle heavy grades, the railcar was ill-designed for New Zealand country runs in that it had insufficient space for luggage, bicycles, dogs and prams; the absence of a lavatory also restricted the duration of runs to which it could be assigned.

The first successful railcars were the Wairarapa type, which were designed to operate on the Rimutaka Incline as part of the Wellington-Masterton-Palmerston North route. These seven cars could each climb the incline in about a third of the time taken by trains powered by the Fell steam locomotives and, of course, did not need to be broken up and then reassembled at each end of the incline section as was the case with carriage trains. The introduction of these forty-nine seat railcars allowed NZR to withdraw steam-hauled expresses from the Wairarapa line. These cars survived until the closure of the incline when the Rimutaka tunnel was completed in 1955.

Two Leyland diesel-electric railcars made their appearance in 1936 on the run between Christchurch and Greymouth, their most important task being to transport copies of The Press to the Coast. These could seat eighteen people, or just eight when laden with newspapers.

* * *

In 1955 when this photograph was taken, the 88-seater class (represented here by RM 101 on the left) had recently entered service and taken over many of the provincial runs operated out of Wellington from the Standard class, represented here by RM 33 on the right. The latter class had been built in 1938-39, and could seat up to fifty-two passengers and travel at up to 100 km/h. Six were built and by mid-1955 they were used mainly on the Wellington-New Plymouth services. The two cars are seen here passing at Manakau, just north of Wellington, on 26 May 1955. (*NZR -- Bob Stott collection*)

The first Standard railcar, Aotea, was built in 1938 and entered service on the Wellington-New Plymouth service in April 1939. In all, six Standards were built at Hutt Workshops. They seated up to fifty-two passengers and were the first railcars to be built with driver cabs at each end, thus eliminating the need for turning after each trip (a design that was to be followed on all subsequent railcar models). They were used on the Wellington-Napier run, and then later the Wellington-New Plymouth and New Plymouth-Taumarunui lines.

The Vulcan railcars, ordered from Britain's Vulcan Foundry in 1938, were known for their speed and acceleration (the first car, RM 50, achieving 130 km/h on its test run). In all, ten were ordered, with one being lost when when a German U-boat torpedoed the cargo ship carrying it to New Zealand. The Vulcans had forty-eight seats. They operated on various lines, including Picton-Christchurch, and were a familiar site on the Otago central line as well as on the Midland line. Vulcans were also used on the west coast of the South Island, between Greymouth and Westport until withdrawn from that line in May 1967. The last Vulcans were removed from NZR service in October 1978. Vulcan railcars have been preserved at the Plains Railway, Tinwald, and the Ferrymead Railway, Christchurch.

The eighty-eight seater articulated railcars were actually built by the Drewry Car Company and the Birmingham Railway Carriages & Wagon Company, with the motors supplied by Fiat (and were variously known as the 'Drewrys', the 'Fiats', the 'articulateds' as well as the 'eighty-eight-seaters'). In all, thirty-five sets were placed in service between March 1955 and May 1958. They were used throughout both islands, operating such services as the evening passenger runs between Christchurch and Dunedin, a daytime return service Dunedin-Invercargill, Gisborne-Wellington (departing at 3.35 am to reach Wellington at 1.50 pm), the run between Auckland and Te Puke in pre-Kaimai tunnel days, through the Rimutaka tunnel on the Woodville-Wellington run, Auckland-Opua, Auckland-Rotorua, Christchurch-Ross, Christchurch-Picton, on the Stillwater-Westport line and Auckland-Okaihau. The articulated cars helped sustain passenger numbers for more than a decade and provided NZR with flexibility not available with the old provincial expresses. By the mid-1960s railcars were operating all long-distance passenger services on other than the main trunk lines in both islands. But the eighty-eight seaters were plagued by mechanical problems for much of their lives, including engine overheating and crankcase wear; toward the end of their life, several fires occurred in the engines.

In addition, their contribution to the arrest of the decline in passenger numbers was short-lived; by the mid-1960s the railcar services were losing money.

NZR withdrew these services from North Auckland, Westport and Te Puke in 1967. By 1971 the Auckland-New Plymouth railcar service had been truncated to just Taumarunui-New Plymouth. In 1973 the fleet had dwindled to twenty-five, three of which were being used for 'Blue Streak' services (which initially operated Auckland-Hamilton but later worked the Auckland-Wellington daytime run). The 'Blue Streak' title was an informal one, due to the two-tone blue (as opposed to traditional red NZR livery) colour scheme for these three units.

An eighty-eight seater railcar painted in its 'Blue Streak' colours motors along near Manakau, the passengers treated to a combination of swaying railcar, underfloor engines going through the gears and the familiar beat as the wheels went over rail joints. (*D.M. Cole — Bob Stott collection*)

When the newer Silver Fern railcars came into service on the NIMT (providing 576 seats a week between Auckland and Wellington, compared with 240 on the thrice-weekly Blue Streak operation), the Blue Streak sets were transferred to the Wellington-New Plymouth run. They were withdrawn from this service on 7 July 1977. The last railcar in New Zealand (other than the Silver Fern sets, detailed below) ran over the Midland line on 10 August 1978.

In 1973 the government said that NZR had been instructed to prepare tender documents for a new generation of provincial railcars. The then Railways Minister, Tom McGuigan, told parliament the new railcars would be fifty-seaters and that at least five sets would be purchased. However, this plan never came to fruition. The motors of the articulated railcar sets were removed and the sets were subsequently re-issued to traffic as blue-coloured Ac carriages to be hauled by locomotives. The last four of these sets were withdrawn from service in April 1985.

The Silver Fern cars consisted of two permanently coupled, 22.8-metre-long, stainless steel cars supplied by a Japanese consortium. Each set could carry ninety-six passengers and they entered service on 14 December 1972. They ran their last Auckland-Wellington service on 1 December 1991, after which the Overlander took over the route. The Silver Fern cars were then transferred to passenger services between Auckland, Tauranga and Rotorua. These services terminated in October 2001. One Silver Fern set is now operated by the tourist service, Dunedin Railways (formerly the Taieri Gorge Railway).

Royal Trains

Early royal tours of New Zealand inevitably involved the use of royal trains: such was the case in 1869 (the Duke of Edinburgh), 1901 (the Duke and Duchess of Cornwall), 1920 (the Prince of Wales), 1927 (the Duke and Duchess of York), 1935 (the Duke of Gloucester) and 1953-54 (Queen Elizabeth II and the Duke of Edinburgh).

On 22 April 1869 a special train was laid on by the Canterbury provincial authorities at Lyttelton to carry Queen Victoria's second son, Prince Alfred, the Duke of Edinburgh, through the tunnel to Christchurch on the then broad-gauge (5ft 3in, or 1,600 mm) track. The Duke returned to his ship three days later, also by special train.

The first substantial train journey, and the first to be called a 'Royal train', was made on 13 June 1901, by the Duke and Duchess of Cornwall (later King George V and Queen Mary). A J class locomotive pulled the five-car train from Auckland to Rotorua, a distance of 274 km; three days later the Royal couple returned along the same route. They later travelled from Wellington to Petone, visiting the then railway workshops at Petone (the Duke also laying the foundation stone of the new NZR head office building in Wellington). Another Royal train conveyed the party, on 25 June 1901, from Christchurch to Dunedin, with civic welcomes held along the route. A pilot train ran ahead of all the Royal specials and an emergency train ran behind them.

Much more extensive use of the NZR system was made by Edward, Prince of Wales, (later Edward VIII and then the Duke of Windsor), in his 1920 visit to the New Zealand. The Prince travelled by rail on the following stretches: Auckland-Rotorua (and return), Auckland-New Plymouth, New Plymouth-Wanganui, Marton-Napier, Napier-Wellington (via Masterton and the Rimutaka Incline) and Wellington-Trentham military camp; in the South Island Royal trains ran Picton-Blenheim, Nelson-Glenhope, Reefton-Hokitika, Arthur's Pass-Christchurch, Christchurch-Dunedin, Dunedin-Invercargill and Invercargill-Lyttelton. Edward travelled on locomotive footplates on two short stretches.

A special carriage was built for the visit of the Duke and Duchess of York (later King George VI and Queen Elizabeth) to New Zealand in 1927. This car, numbered 1617, had a rounded end with observation windows. It was built to a reduced width to allow it to pass through narrow cuttings on some branch lines. The sitting area, sited at the end of the car with entrance doors on either side, had a large sofa and easy chairs, and a side corridor provided access to two bedrooms and a shower, while a kitchen was located at the opposite end. The inside of the car was finished with polished mahogany, and there were electric fans and cigar lighters. The Auckland to Rotorua journey was again the first train trip taken on a Royal tour, after which the couple travelled by road to National Park to rejoin their train. Again, too, the isolated Picton and Nelson sections were used by the Royal party, with the Duke joining the Royal train at Inangahua, travelling to Hokitika and Greymouth before going on to Christchurch (the Otira tunnel was open by this time). He travelled by rail to Dunedin, then up the Otago Central line to its terminus at Cromwell, by road and lake steamer to Kingston, and on (via the Kingston and Waimea Plains lines) to Gore and Invercargill. The train's final stretch took the Duke to join his ship at Bluff.

Prince Henry, Duke of Gloucester, boarded his NZR Royal train on 19 December 1934 at Wellington's old Thorndon station for a trip to Napier, having two days earlier laid the foundation stone for the present Wellington railway station. The Duke rejoined his train at Rotorua for the journey to Auckland. He subsequently travelled between Auckland and National Park, Hunterville-New Plymouth (via the Okahukura-Stratford line), New Plymouth-Wanganui, Palmerston North-Wellington (via the Wairarapa line), Greymouth-Ross, Ross-Dunedin, Dunedin-Invercargill, Invercargill-Lumsden and Lumsden-Kingston.

Car 1617, built for the 1927 tour, was used again on South Island portion of the 1953-54 tour by Elizabeth II and the Duke of Edinburgh; the consist also included car 1655, built in 1929 at the Addington workshops as the general manager's touring carriage. This latter car had lounges and a dining table that could seat six. (Both cars ended their days at Arthur's Pass where, their wheels removed, they were spotted in 1974 after having been written off. They were being used by the Railway Welfare Society). The Queen first joined the Royal train on 7 January 1954, when she travelled from Hastings to Palmerston North. The new De class diesels were used on the Hastings-Palmerston North-New Plymouth and the Wellington-Summit sections of the Royal tour.

Stock Trains

Cartage of livestock, particularly sheep, was once one of the mainstays of NZR goods services. Hundreds of stations were equipped with their stock pens and loading banks, and the ubiquitous four-wheeler, double-deck sheep wagons were a feature of the railway scene throughout the country. The rail was vital to farmers for bringing in new stock or dispatching it to the works. For example, before Gisborne was connected to the national rail network, it was common for finished sheep to be railed up the then Gisborne section (later Moutohora branch), then trekked across the intervening hills to the rail terminal at Taneatua in the Bay of Plenty, whence they were railed to the Horotiu or Westfield freezing works. However, once Gisborne was connected to the main system, a large stock sale yard grew at Matawhero, just south of the city, with the animals being railed to Napier and beyond.

Over the years vast numbers of varying types of rolling stock were built to carry animals around the NZR system. For example, there were the H class, four-wheeled cattle wagons, some of which were built between 1939 and 1942. They were built with extra wide doors, so they could carry an elephant for circus trains should the need arise. In normal traffic use, these wagons could accommodate eight cattle. The J class double-decker sheep wagons could hold 80 animals.

But from the 1950s the development of larger lorries, followed by the gradual deregulation of road transport, effectively brought about the demise of cartage of animals on the NZR system. Toward the end it was a dramatic decline: in 1962 NZR carted 804,461 cattle, 725,624 calves, 7,001,265 sheep and 420,161 pigs. But by 1975 the figures had fallen away to 96,702 cattle, 283,705 calves, 522,100 sheep and 48,080 pigs.

In 1975 then Minister of Railways Ron Bailey said it would be government policy to phase out livestock cartage because it was uneconomic, partly as it was usually a one-way traffic.

In recent years Tranz Rail experimented with carrying livestock within a few intermodal 'crates', but nothing came of this because meat works had long removed their rail sidings. In April 1994, for example, trial runs were made carrying lambs in sheep containers; one shipment consisted of 1,000 animals from Invercargill to Dunedin, another travelling from Dunedin to Timaru.

Suburban Trains

Cities with suburban services: Auckland, Wellington, Christchurch, Dunedin, and Invercargill.

Status: Auckland and Wellington — operating.
      Christchurch — withdrawn 2 February 1972.
      Dunedin — withdrawn 3 December 1982.
      Invercargill — withdrawn 1967.

Trains ran for many years between Napier and Hastings. Although these both grew as separate cities (with their own evening newspapers), these services were essentially suburban in nature. The train frequency was significantly reduced in 1926 when NZR started a parallel bus service. The trains ceased altogether a few years later.

Modern train, modern-looking city: a suburban working on the newly electrified Auckland system. (*Roy Sinclair*)

In the 1961-62 year NZR reported 23,311,438 suburban passenger journeys. By this time, however, suburban services were one of the biggest loss-makers on NZR's books. A 1979 report from NZR, Time for Change, revealed the extent of the losses. Wellington revenue from suburban passengers was meeting only twenty-six per cent of operating costs. Dunedin was only slightly better at twenty-eight per cent, with Auckland fares covering forty-six per cent of operating costs.

The most complex of the suburban operations is Wellington's, where four lines are in use: on the North Island Main Trunk as far as Waikanae, on the Wairarapa line as far as Upper Hutt (for electric multiple units) and Masterton (locomotive-hauled commuter trains) and on the Johnsonville and Melling branches. (The suburban train service also included the Te Aro line until its closure in 1917. In the present day the Capital Connection to Palmerston North and the services from the Wairarapa into the capital are classed as commuter trains, rather than being strictly speaking suburban workings.)

It was Wellington, in fact, that saw the first suburban passenger services with the introduction in 1897 of workers' tickets at concessional rates, These were made available for travel between the capital and stations in the Hutt Valley; the following year the special tickets were extended to Auckland, Christchurch and Dunedin.

In 1881 six trains ran daily between Wellington and Lower Hutt, but by 1900 this number had grown nearly threefold (although some of these were mixed trains, which shunted en route at Petone or Ngauranga), All lines around the main towns, and then cities, were built to provide passenger services as well as carry goods. But the first railway extension made specifically to serve suburban passengers was the lengthening of the branch from Petone to Waterloo, The original line, while a more direct route to Upper Hutt, skirted the sparsely populated western side of the Hutt Valley, and from the end of World War II the large flood plain of the lower valley was being rapidly subdivided and urbanised, By April 1947 passenger trains were running to the new railhead at Taita.

Recent years have seen Auckland, first, be issued in the 1990s with surplus diesel multiple units bought from West Australian Government Railways and, now, equipped with especially built electric trains. But, for most of rail's history in New Zealand,

Wellington was the only city to see rolling stock designed exclusively for suburban use: these were electric multiple units from English Electric, introduced in 1938. However, the electric multiple units could not cope with peak-hour traffic on either Hutt Valley or Paekakariki services, and they were supplemented by consists of old open-platform wooden carriages hauled by electric locomotives. A typical train from, for example, Taita could include a combination of old express cars with lavatories, old first-class cars with green leather seating and a variety of second-class cars, some with more rudimentary wooden seats. On the morning journeys, the first few carriages were packed because they were closest on arrival to the concourse at Wellington station and also gave those passengers a head start for trams and buses taking workers further into the capital's business area, It was also common for travellers from Taita, the originating station for these services, to have their 'regular seats' in those front carriages.

In November 1981 the first shipment arrived in Wellington of the forty-four sets of two-coach units from Ganz-Mavag in Hungary. These were bigger than the old English Electric sets, with more comfortable seating and brighter lighting.

Until the decision was made in the present century to electrify rail lines in Auckland, the northern city — in terms of local trains services — had always appeared to be the poor cousin when it came to suburban train services. Even as late as the early 1960s, when Wellingtonians travelled on electric units or electric locomotive-hauled trains, Aucklanders were still travelling behind Wab steam locomotives. Again, in 1983, train services were cut back in Auckland, with twenty-six of the 108 operations being cancelled. At the time there were estimated to be about 4,000 people using the Auckland services each day. Passenger services on the Onehunga branch, which had been declining in importance since trams started running to the area in 1903, were withdrawn by 1964. The train from Auckland to Mercer, known as the Mercer Local, was withdrawn in 1967.

Christchurch also had a distinct suburban service covering the 9.8 km to and from Lyttelton, which survived until 1972. The then Minister of Railways, John ('Peter') Gordon, said the trains were being withdrawn because few were carrying more than a busload of passengers, and annual numbers in 1971 were down one million on the 1963-64 year. Christchurch also had other services that were adjuncts to suburban operations. In the 1940s, for example, there were trains northwards and south-wards from Christchurch to Waipara and Ashburton respec-tively, while two morning workers' trains ran from Rangiora, with return services in the afternoon. Late afternoon on a typi-cal day saw — apart from Lyttelton services — trains pulling out for Waipara at 4.37 pm, for Ashburton at 5.05 pm and then the Rangiora local at 5.17 pm.

Dunedin had suburban trains running to Port Chalmers and Mosgiel, the latter connecting with services on the Outram. There was also at one stage a Vulcan railcar stabled at Palmerston overnight which provided a daily morning train into Dunedin, serving all the small wayside stations such Warrington, The Gums and Osborne, which had no other public transport ser-vice; it returned to Palmerston late afternoon. In the 1950s there were twelve trains each way between Mosgiel and Dunedin on weekdays, but by 1982 this was down to three inward and two outward trains a day.

A suburban train service also ran between Invercargill and Bluff until withdrawn in 1967, with school trains and workers' trains at peak hours. As noted elsewhere, in 1929 the sole Clayton steam railcar was used for suburban services to and from Bluff, but increasingly mixed trains took up many of the services as passenger numbers declined. In one enterprising move by NZR people in Invercargill, in the 1930s a Shopper's Special from Edendale and return was introduced to bring country people into the city for Friday night shopping.

Boat Trains

Last boat train: Ran Christchurch to Lyttleton on 14 September 1976 for the passengers catching the ferry Rangatira for Wellington.

The Lyttelton boat trains were once part of the travelling experience for New Zealanders moving between the two islands in the era before air transport was used by the mass of travellers and the introduction of the rail ferries between Picton and Wellington. Each morning, as the Union Steam Ship Company ferries made their way up Lyttelton harbour for arrival at 7.00 am, passengers would begin queuing with their luggage at the gangway entrances, ready to make the dash to secure seats on the train waiting at the wharf.

The carriages had been heated by means of a steam locomotive being coupled and pumping hot water through the pipes lining each car; that engine would be replaced by an electric locomotive for the journey through the Lyttelton tunnel to Christchurch. The boat train had both first and second class carriages and the paper boys selling the Christchurch morning paper, The Press, did brisk business as they walked through the train. For those travelling in the opposite direction in the evening, there was no separate boat train: the express from Invercargill ran through to the ferry wharf.

However, even before the demise of the inter-island ferry service, the boat train was a shadow of its former self. An unhappy (for the boat train) conjunction of events meant its end: air transport had become more affordable, the ferry service had been disrupted (the sinking of the Wahine in 1968 meant the end of a six-day service in both directions); much business had disappeared from 1962 when NZR began operating rail/road ferries between Wellington and Picton; and the opening of the road tunnel under the Port Hills between Lyttelton and Christchurch meant many passengers were now met at the wharf by friends and relations who could drive to the port.

Another port served by boat trains was Picton. The ferry Tamahine, which had begun the Wellington-Picton ferry service in 1925 (and would continue in that role until 1962), would be met by two trains standing at the wharf — a non-stop passenger service to Blenheim and, running behind it, an all-stops mixed train. Timetables for 1938 showed that the Tamahine departed Wellington at 2.15 pm and arrived in Picton at 6.20 pm. In 1956 the boat trains were placed by the eighty-eight seater Fiat railcars but this service last only four years, the railcars being replaced by buses to Blenheim (although until 1964 the north-bound railcars from Christchurch would still run right through to the wharf).

In Auckland, after the Onehunga branch was extended to the wharf there in 1878, boat trains operated to serve passengers using the steamers that plied between Onehunga port and New Plymouth. At one stage NZR also operated special trains to meet mail steamers arriving at Bluff from Australia, whipping the mail and passengers into Invercargill.

3
Rails That Built a Nation

RAILWAYS WERE BUILT TO help areas as they were opened up to European settlement. Almost all the first lines terminated at a port, thus establishing a transport system for wool and other primary exports. It is surprising how little things have changed in that regard at the beginning of the twenty-first century — the rail system's financial health is still heavily dependent on carting exports to the main ports, with logs and coal being hauled in volumes that would not have been conceivable more than 100 years ago. Thus, the Midland line in the South Island would probably not survive in today's transport world but for the coal being transported from the West Coast for shipment at Lyttelton. The Port of Tauranga took the concept further by establishing an inland port in South Auckland, with goods carried to and from its wharves by rail.

While the ports were one end of the system, at the other was the network of branch lines ending at country stations that often consisted of little more than a few buildings surrounded by bush or paddocks but, again, they were conceived often as a means of opening up country rather than being justifiable on the grounds of pure transport economics.

Fortunately the gauge question was settled very early in the piece in New Zealand, unlike across in the Australian colonies where three gauges still exist. This early resolution in New Zealand was possible because, unlike in Australia, there was a central government, and the provincial governments were dissolved in 1876. Initially, though, Canterbury had built its first line to the Irish gauge of 5 ft 3 in (1,600mm), Otago and Auckland had adopted the British standard gauge of 4ft 8½ (1,435mm). But the central government was, with the passing of the Public Works Policy Act 1870, able to impose the narrow gauge of 3ft 6in (1,067mm). Many in the provinces fought to retain their own gauges — one can only read this with horror as to the consequences had they been successful — but fortunately one politician was able to lend valuable support to Wellington's case. James Crowe Richmond had been a member of the Taranaki Provincial Council and then moved to national politics in the 1860s as colonial secretary. However his most useful experience was that he had been in railway engineering, having worked for Isambard Kingdom Brunel, the great British railway builder. He led the case for the adoption of the narrow gauge, arguing that with a population of just 250,000 people (the Maori population was not counted) the narrow gauge would be the cheapest option.

In 1870, with Julius Vogel newly installed as the Colonial Treasurer, just 74 km of railway line was open for traffic throughout the colony; but by 1879 the state railway system had grown to 1,902 km. Speaking in the House of Representatives in June 1870, Vogel spelled out his vision of a line running from Nelson to Hokitika, via Westport and Greymouth, and also one making its way down the South Island from Picton,

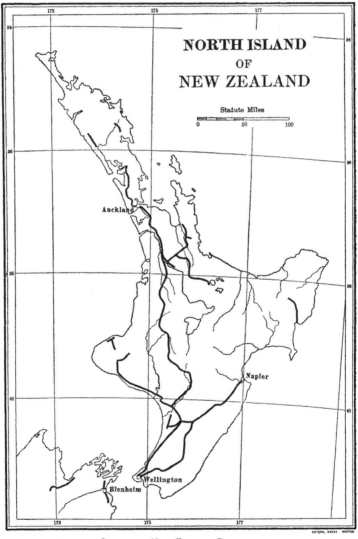

SKETCH OF NEW ZEALAND RAILWAYS

These maps of the New Zealand rail system as at 1909 show how many isolated sections remained (*the railways are in bold, the rivers systems in grey*). In the North Island the main trunk had been completed in 1908 but the provincial centres of Gisborne and New Plymouth were not connected to the main network. In the South Island, the gap between Christchurch and Blenheim would not be ended until 1945, while the Midland line westward from Christchurch would be completed in 1923.

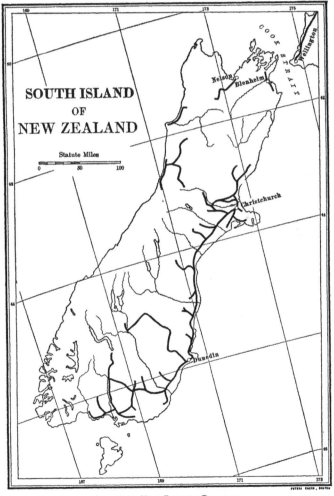

SKETCH OF NEW ZEALAND RAILWAYS

eventually reaching Bluff. His scheme would eventually come to involve borrowing £10　million to build lines at the lowest feasible cost. Vogel envisaged trains having a maximum speed of twenty miles an hour, thus allowing cheaper light rails to be used. The railway construction was authorised by the Immigration and Public Works Act 1870, this legislation providing for the use of 2.5 million acres and £7.5 million to develop a railway system. The act also created the Public Works Department, the agency that was to supervise the construction of most of what would become the NZR national network. Initially, Vogel authorised the Otago and Canterbury provincial governments to undertake construction, with the central government to reimburse them upon completion. Private companies were also allowed, and this led to the building of several lines, such as the Methven and Waimea Plains branches.

By 1880 much had been achieved in the South Island: on the east coast the Picton-Blenheim line was open, and the main trunk had been constructed between Waipara in North Canterbury and Bluff, along with the first stages of many branch lines.

In the North Island, trains were running from Wellington through to Upper Hutt and over the Rimutaka Ranges to Masterton (with the Woodside-Greytown branch also open). Auckland's rail system had gone north as far as Helensville and had penetrated south to Te Awamutu. Taranaki had its then main line between New Plymouth and Waitara, but the rails had also been laid as far as Ngaere on what would become the connection to Wellington via Marton. In the other direction, rails had been laid from Paxton, via Palmerston North and Wanganui, to Waitotara, while Hawke's Bay had a railway southwards from

Napier as far as Makotuku and to Ahuriri from 1874 in the other direction. In the far north, two small sections had been completed by 1880: between Whangarei and Kamo, and Kawakawa and Taumarere. In Auckland the line from the city to Onehunga had been opened in 1873.

Isolated sections were a common feature of the New Zealand railway system in its first seventy-five years of existence. In 1900 there were still ten separate sections of railway in New Zealand totalling 3,200 km in length.

By 1914, after four decades of railway construction and expansion including the completion of the North Island Main Trunk, there were still a considerable number of isolated sections on the NZR system: Dargaville-Kaihu, Whangarei-Opua, Gisborne-Otoko, Nelson-Glenhope, Ross-Otira, Westport-Mokihinui Mine and Picton-Ward. After the end of the First World War, the remaining main towns were connected to the main network: Greymouth in 1923 (with the completion of the Otira tunnel), Whangarei in 1925, Tauranga in 1928, Dargaville and Gisborne in 1942, Westport in 1943 and Blenheim in 1945. In addition, New Plymouth obtained a direct link to Auckland in 1933 with the completion of the Stratford-Okahukura line. Thus, the railway network did not reach all the major towns until 1945 (and, even then, Nelson was still isolated from the trunk system).

A report published in *New Zealand Railways Magazine* in 1926 show that, not only were isolated sections a great inconvenience, they were a drain on railway finances. In the financial year to 31 March 1926, the Kaihu branch in Northland (38.5 km) earned £8,411 and was still £10,870 in the red; Gisborne section (96.5 km) brought in £39,565 in goods and passenger income but lost £37,219; the Nelson section earned £28,281 but was in the red to the tune of £26,740, while the Picton section earned £42,352, nowhere near enough to cover its costs, posting a loss of £30,938 for the year.

Many railway lines in New Zealand are now footnotes in history. But their stories, whether they be part of the trunk system or a rural branch that never saw anything more glamorous than a slow mixed three days a week, are part of New Zealand railway lore.

North Island Main Trunk

Length: 680.76 km
Opened: 6 November 1908
Passenger services: Scenic tourist trains between Wellington and Auckland; suburban rail services in Auckland and Wellington; daily return service Palmerston North-Wellington.
Electrification: Auckland and Wellington surburban lines, Te Rapa-Palmerston North

The North Island Main Trunk took more than forty years to build. Of that period, the most difficult part — through the mountainous terrain between Marton and Te Awamutu in the centre of the island — required twenty-five years to complete. The route eventually chosen was not without its opponents. In 1874 a survey was carried out on a route which would have' taken the line through Taupo. Sir George Grey, the Governor, argued for a route via Taranaki. Almost all the possible routes involved the consent of Maori landowners.

The idea of the main trunk had been a live one since 1863 when the Auckland Provincial Council decided to build a line out to Drury; the main purpose was to help enable the subduing of the Maori in the Waikato but it was also seen as the first stage of a line reaching Wellington

The section from Rangiriri to Ngaruawahia (then called Newcastle), a distance of 29 km, was built using the Engineer Volunteer Militia. Those enrolling received a minimum of six shillings and three hot meals a day, but the work was hard as they pressed into what was still very much frontier territory after the tribes had been beaten back into the King Country by imperial forces. Days began with an hour's drill, and work on the line spanned twelve hours from 6.00 am, with two ninety-minute breaks. The militia wore blue serge uniforms and the men were subject to military discipline. The first men were enrolled in December 1873, and the section they built was opened to traffic on 13 August 1877. The inaugural train that day consisted of three F class locomotives handing twenty-four or six-wheeler cars. The line reached Frankton by December and Te Awamutu by 1880, where work halted until negotiations could be completed with the powerful chiefs of the King Country.

I

In 1882 Parliament passed the North Island Main Trunk Loan Act, which authorised the raising of £1 million. No route was specified and the Government Surveyor, John Rochfort, conducted four treks over the central region to find the best one. He had to deal with hostile Maori along the way, particularly the

Patutokotoko tribe; they held him for three days and threatened to kill him if he returned. His eventual report recommended a central route that was largely built as he had proposed.

The greatest surveying and engineering achievement on a railway project replete with challenges was the Raurimu Spiral, conceived by Robert West Holmes, senior engineer at the Public Works Department. It includes within its 25 km-length two tunnels (of 96 metres and 384 metres respectively), three horseshoe curves and a complete circle, allowing trains to climb to or descend from a height of 550 metres in a rugged landscape via a track that overlaps itself and essentially goes around in a circle. The northern side of the Waimarino Plateau involved the line dropping the 550 metres in the space of 27.5 km. It was not possible to go around the problem, as all the alternatives would have involved huge costs; one such alternative would have required nine viaducts. Holmes, after considering various options, hit upon the spiral plan, allowing a grade no more arduous than 1 in 50. The 94-ton X-class steam locomotive was designed to handle the steep grades of the NIMT and some of these locomotives were permanently based at Taumarunui to help pull trains up the spiral. Nevertheless, it could take a steam-hauled train forty minutes to climb the spiral, the time being halved when diesel-electric traction was introduced. The Raurimu Spiral remains an essential part of the NIMT; no one has ever been able to come up with a better idea for surmounting the challenge of this physical landscape.

The first sod for the line south of Te Awamutu was turned in April 1885. By 1904 the two railheads were still 146 km apart, and bad weather impeded work even beyond those delays allowed due to the nature of the terrain. This final section included several imposing viaducts, such as the Makatote, Hapuawhenua and Taonui, with the contracts for those being let only as late as 1905. From 1906 the workforce on the line grew to about 2,500 as the government became increasingly concerned over progress. By late 1907, under pressure William Hall-Jones, who held both the public works and railways portfolios, a night shift was added to the roster, the men working by kerosene lamps. The Seddon Government had, in 1903, assured the House of Representatives that the NIMT would be open to traffic by 1908. By May of that year Public Works trains were able to run on all but 24 km of the trunk line, the gap being between Makatote viaduct and Ohakune station. The last rails were laid three months before the driving of the final spike ceremony, and work on the last of the viaducts was completed in July 1908.

The completion of the North Island Main Trunk between Palmerston North and Auckland made it imperative that the Wellington and Manawatu Company line be taken under NZR control as it controlled the section of the line south from Palmerston North to Wellington, an intolerable operational situation. The shareholders were bought out in 1908 for a total of £933,000, regarded as a bargain for the government,

In its first year of operation the completed NIMT saw relatively light traffic over the central section of the line by comparison with later times; between Marton and Taihape, for example, three mixed trains and two goods trains ran each way daily. By the middle of the twentieth century the line was often working close to capacity to accommodate two night express trains in each direction, as well as many heavy goods trains. In the years between 1952 and 1974 traffic density on the Marton-Taihape section more than doubled.

Before the Tawa deviation opened to passenger trains in 1937, the last section of the mainline approach to Wellington was a slow business. In 1933 an Ab class locomotive hauls the Auckland-Wellington Limited express through the winding Ngaio Gorge. After the deviation was built, the old line became the Johnsonville branch, used as part of the capital's suburban system. (*NZR—Bob Stott collection*)

In July 1967 the line was fully dieselised after the floors of the tunnels between Pukerua Bay and Paekakariki (just north of

Wellington) were lowered to allow Da locomotives to work right through to Wellington. Before that, the Wellington-Paekakariki section was operated using electric locomotives from 1940, with the time-consuming business of attaching or uncoupling steam or diesel locomotives at the latter station swhich hauled the trains over the rest of the NIMT.

The line was electrified between Wellington and Paekakariki by June 1940 and extended to Paraparaumu on 8 May 1983, with the electrification extended to Waikanae. The central section of the NIMT was electrified by May 1988 after a study had shown that electric traction would allow faster and heavier trains to run through the central section with all its difficult terrain. That 1974 study had concluded that while a diesel-electric locomotive could haul 720 tonnes at 27 km/h on the Raurimu Spiral, an electric locomotive would be able to pull between 1,100 tonnes and 1,200 tonnes at 45 km/h over the same section; overall, it was estimated that electrification of the central section would slice three hours of a journey between Auckland and Wellington.

East Coast Main Trunk

Length: 181.32 km to present terminus at Kawerau
Opened: 2 September 1928 (on original route)
Passenger traffic: Railcar services survived as far as Tauranga until 7 October 2001, when the Kaimai Express was withdrawn.
Status: As described by the New Zealand Geographic Board, the East Coast Main Trunk now runs between Hamilton and Kawerau with a disused branch line to Taneatua from the junc-

tion at Hawkens. Originally the continuation of the railway line from Taneatua was to be extended to Opotiki, on through the Waioeka Gorge to Gisborne, linking to the Palmerston North–Gisborne line. Work did begin, however due to two world wars, an economic depression and an influenza epidemic, this ambitious extension of the railway line was never completed.

The East Coast Main Trunk has had a number of forms over its life. The title was first used in 1928 when rails to the intended terminus at Taneatua. At that stage its route went via the Karangahake Gorge, a narrow gorge with the line going through a 1,006 metre tunnel and over various bridges as it would through the natural break in the ranges this section being bypassed with the opening of the Kaimai Tunnel in 1978). The other main engineering work was the bridge over Tauranga Harbour, 411 metres long and consisting of fourteen spans — it is the longest bridge on the North Island system.

Early travellers on the line needed much patience: in the months after the completion of the route, those boarding the train at Taneatua for the 6.25 am departure knew they were scheduled to arrive in Auckland at 11.02 pm that evening. They changed trains at Tauranga, Paeroa, Morrinsville and Frankton. On the return journey it was necessary to spend the night at Tauranga. By the end of 1928 the latter became a same-day trip but from Paeroa to Taneatua passengers travelled in a mixed train, that is, a goods train with car or cars attached.

By 1951 the timing of the Auckland-Taneatua service was reduced to six hours by eliminating stops at the smaller stations but frequency was also reduced — to two trains a week. Then in 1959 all passenger services terminated at Te Puke, with daily runs by eighty-eight seater railcars providing a service. These, however, were withdrawn in 1967. It was not until December 1991 that railcar services returned as far as Tauranga in the form of the Kaimai Express.

The East Coast Main Trunk was always a busy goods line. Even before the opening of the Port of Tauranga and the construction of the huge Kinleith pulp mill, tonnages between Taneatua and Waihi had trebled between 1928 and the early 1950s. The forests of the region were always an important factor in the line's operations. In 1925 the National Timber Company built the Matahina Tramway, connecting with the NZR at Edgecumbe; then from 1939 the Whakatane Board Mills plant added to the freight task. In 1957, the rails reached further into the forests with the opening of the Murupara branch. Another new branch, to Kinleith, also generated an enormous new traffic load of forest products.

The East Coast Main Trunk's terminus at Kawerau in 1982 was proclaimed the busiest station on the NZR system in freight volume terms.

Palmerston North–Gisborne

Length: 390.4 km
Opened: 1 February 1943
Passenger Services: Withdrawn from 7 October 2001 when Bay Express ceased services between Wellington and Napier
Status: Open to Napier. The Napier-Gisborne section was closed and mothballed in October 2012 after washouts destroyed sections of track.

It's late 1886 and much of Palmerston North turns out to greet the first train to arrive from Wellington soon after the last spike was driven to complete the line built by the Wellington and Manawatu Railway Company. (*Alan Bellamy collection*)

The railway to Gisborne is really two separate sections: the Hawke's Bay line from Palmerston North to Napier completed in 1891 and, secondly, the Gisborne section finished during the Second World War. It was a significant project because, unlike in the South Island, rail development in the North Island had been delayed by the Land Wars between the Maori and the British colonial authorities. Indeed, before the Napier-Hastings section was completed, the North Island had only two other railways: the Auckland-Onehunga and Wellington-Lower Hutt sections.

As with other lines, the railhead advanced gradually — to
Waipukurau by 1 September 1876, then to Woodville (156.2
km from Napier) on 22 March 1887.

The Gisborne line north of Napier with a typical goods train of
the steam era — a rake of sheep wagons, open wagons and covered vans. This train was spotted near the small wayside station
of Eskdale. (*Bob Stott*)

Then came the greatest engineering challenge on the

Hawke's Bay line: the Manawatu Gorge between Woodville and Palmerston North. New Zealand's topography is such that railway builders often found that the most efficient route through rugged or mountainous terrain was to follow the river gorges. And, ever since, these gorges have offered some of the most spectacular scenery for the rail traveller. Three hundred men were employed to carve a track-bed from the rock walls along the 8 km gorge, the task including five short tunnels and twenty-six bridges. Finally, the line reached Palmerston North in 1891 (further delays having been caused by one contractor going bankrupt) and services from Napier connected with trains operated from the capital by the Wellington and Manawatu Railway Company. Henceforth a passenger could depart Napier at 10.45 am and be on the Manawatu company's Wellington platform (Thorndon station) by 9.50 pm.

Meanwhile, another thirty-two years were to pass before Gisborne was connected to the NZR network. Work began in 1912 laying track north of Napier but then progress was hampered by delays: the First World War, floods, the Great Depression — and, not least, by the Napier earthquake of 3 February 1931, New Zealand's deadliest earthquake devastated the cities of Napier and Hastings. At least 256 people died in the magnitude 7.8 earthquake and part of the new line was destroyed and not re-opened until October 1936. Then the project caught a break. In late 1935, New Zealand's first Labour government was elected; by early 1936 the order went out to restart work on the Gisborne section. The railway line reached Ruapunga in February 1937; by August that year a nightly goods train was running to Wairoa, the main town between Napier and Gisborne. A month earlier a railcar ran a ministerial special to Wairoa, stopping at the Mohaka viaduct where Public Works Minister Bob Semple officially opened the structure, the highest railway bridge in New Zealand and Australia at 97 metres above stream level. Semple told the small crowd that the line from Napier to Wairoa had cost £2,590,000, a massive sum in the depression era, and added: 'The line was born to trouble, and it has had a hard passage all the way'.

But more trouble was to follow. Part of the line was damaged by floods in 1938 and closed for seven months. The terrain through which the line had been built would be forever a challenge for track maintenance gangs. In 2012 washouts closed the line again. The subsequent decision to mothball the line was no doubt made easier by the dramatic decline in revenue in recent years. But what must be remembered is just what a lifeline to this part of eastern New Zealand the line has been. The 1954 NZR annual report shows that 18,317 passenger tickets were bought at Gisborne in the preceding year, 39,658 at Wairoa, a respectable 4,542 at Nuhaka and 2,179 at Ruapunga. But, of course, on top of this business there were all the tickets sold to people boarding at the smaller wayside stations; the 1959 passenger timetable shows that the railcars, after leaving Gisborne and pausing on the outskirts of that city at Matawhero, would pick up passengers not only at the large stations mentioned above but at Muriwai, Maraetaha, Bartletts, Kopuawhara, Opoutama, Waikokopu, Whakaki, Tuhara, Ohinepaka, Waihua, Kotemaori, Putorino, Kahika, Tutira, Waipunga, Eskdale, Bay

View and Westshore—and that was just as far as Napier. Then south of Napier the railcars had many more stops before reaching Wellington.

Stratford–Okahukura Line

Length: 143.49 km.
Opened: 4 September 1933.
Passenger services: Withdrawn 24 January 1983.
Status: Mothballed by KiwiRail after derailment caused track damage. Now used by a tourism group to run small rail carts for visitors.

The government had planned as early as 1878 to build a line that would provide New Plymouth with a more direct link to the Waikato and Auckland, and Taranaki interests lobbied for many years to have the NIMT routed via Stratford rather than the more direct route through the centre of the North Island that was eventually chosen. By 1888 surveys were under way to connect New Plymouth.

In 1900 the government moved to authorise a line starting from Stratford, and by 9 August 1902 the branch to Toko was opened to traffic. The extension to Oruru, later Douglas, was opened on 1 March 1905, a distance of 17.85 km from Stratford. Work continued, with the railhead reaching Huiroa, then the work gangs pressed on to Te Wera, their task including the Kiore tunnel, the first of twenty-four to be built before the rails could reach the NIMT. The need for this and two other tunnels, along with swampy conditions, meant that the railhead did not each Whangamomona, a distance of 60.4 km, until 1 July 1914.

In 1911 work had begun from the other end of the route. Then, in 1923, men who were on relief schemes for the unemployed and the Public Works Department began operating trains from Okahukura to Ohura in 1926. The following year work was stepped up from the other end and soon nine tunnels were concurrently under construction.

By 1931 the two sections were just 18.5 km apart. Fortunately for the project, it was so near completion by this time that the Great Depression did not take its toll as it did with many other uncompleted railway lines; this particular project was pressed on to completion rather than being abandoned when the money dried up. By November 1932 the two railheads met near Heao, with the completed line being handed over to NZR control on 4 September 1933.

Apart from attracting local traffic and allowing New Pymouth a more direct rail route to Auckland, the completion of the line allowed NZR greater flexibility when there were any problems or blockages on the central section of the NIMT. This was illustrated most dramatically after the 1953 Tangiwai disaster when traffic was diverted around the damaged section of the main trunk, the central section of the trunk being out of commission, so trains were able to move between Wellington and Auckland by means of a detour through Taranaki province, diverting at Marton and travelling to Stratford on the New Plymouth line, then running across to Okahukura.

The refreshment rooms (the separate building nearest the camera) have been long closed as J 1205 waits at Whangamomona's platform, while a goods train headed in the opposite direction sits on the loop until cleared to move back on to the single track main line. This locomotive was built in 1939 by North British Locomotive Company of Glasgow and written off in 1967. (*Bob Stott*)

In 1956 the express passenger trains on the line were replaced by the eighty-eight seater railcars running between Auckland New Plymouth. In 1971, the railcar runs were truncated to operate between New Plymouth and Taumarunui. Mixed trains disappeared in 1975.

Wairarapa Line

Length: 171.5 km between Wellington and Woodville. Duplicated 29.4 km Wellington-Trentham.
Opened: 2 August 1897
Passenger Traffic: Withdrawn from Masterton-Woodville section in 1988. Commuter trains originate from Masterton in the Wairarapa as well as by electric multiple units from Upper Hutt and Taita, all running to terminate at Wellington.

This line runs from Wellington via the Hutt Valley, the Rimutaka tunnel (which superseded the Rimutaka Incline over the range), and through the Wairarapa to Woodville. The section to Lower Hutt was opened to traffic on 14 April 1874, the departure of first train being witnessed by twenty European men and two Maori women, according to The Evening Post. The Wellington Independent saw the line as the first stage of 'a grand trunk route' to Auckland.

Upper Hutt, at the top of the Hutt Valley, was reached on 1 February 1876. Then the builders had to tackle the imposing Rimutaka Ranges.

It was one thing to build a railway up the Hutt Valley to Upper Hutt, it was quite another to surmount the Rimutakas, especially the very steep Wairarapa side. When that section of line was completed, the Upper Hutt-Featherston journey involved trains negotiating 148 curves.

This classic photograph shows the Rimutaka Incline at its most dramatic — the Fell engines placed strategically along a lengthy passenger consist, all working hard to control the train on this steep line. This shows the train at Siberia Curve with the fence built to break the violent winds, a frequent occurance. The fence was built after a gust swept part of a train off the rails in 1880 with three children being killed. (*NZR—Bob Stott collection*)

Trains began with a 1-in-38 climb out of Upper Hutt into the Mangaroa Valley, followed by a 1-in-43 gradient to the Kaitoke Saddle. Then it was a 1-in-42 grade to the summit. Then the hard work really began: the planners had no way of getting around the reality of a 1-in-14 gradient on the Wairarapa side. The only feasible means of negotiating that fact of life was to adopt the system devised by the English engineer John Barra-clough Fell. This involved a centre rail, sitting above the level of the outside rails, already used successfully in the French Alps and in Brazil. Fell's locomotives, as well as the conventional side wheels, had horizontal wheels that gripped the centre rail. This system ensured sufficient traction to climb a very steep grade; and, with horizontal wheels (also attached to the brake vans) there was sufficient braking capacity to control the trains on descent. Between Cross Creek and Summit the trains climbed 265 metres in the space of 5 km. The Fell engines ordered for the construction and operation of the incline never needed replacing, surviving seventy-seven years of hard labour until closure of the incline.

The main shortcoming was the time involved in breaking up trains both at Summit and Cross Creek in order to place and then remove the four or five Fell engines from their positions all along the train. Going uphill there would be one in the lead and the remainder coupled at regular intervals along the consist; on the downhill trip the engines could be coupled together at the front. The heaviest trains also required five Fell brake vans. This, and the slow speeds of 10 km/h on the incline, meant that a journey between Wellington and Masterton could take a very long time; for example, the afternoon train from the capital left Te Aro station at 3.50 pm and reached Masterton at 8.25 pm. By comparison, the 5.30 pm commuter train from Wellington in 2014 now reaches Masterton in one hour, forty-three minutes. The 28 km journey over the Rimutakas in 1901 from Kaitoke to Featherston took one hour, twelve minutes to negotiate.

With up to five locomotives spilled throughout the consist, a single train on the incline could have as many as sixteen men crewing it (ten engine crew and six guards). The incline required constant maintenance by track gangs. There were three tunnels along its length. A windbreak fence was installed at Siberia Curve after a train was blown from the line in 1880 and three children killed.

Two of the key stations generated no traffic other than from the railway workers living there. Summit did not even have a station building, just a signal box and railway houses, while Cross Creek had a rudimentary shelter but no other facilities for passengers. Cross Creek did, however, possess large engine sheds and other facilities needed to maintain and fuel the Fell locomotives, along with a school and house for the resident teacher.

Until 1908, when the government acquired the Wellington and Manawatu Railway Company together with its coastal line between the capital and Palmerston North, all NZR traffic in and out of Wellington had to be routed over the incline. As soon as the private company was purchased, NZR was thereafter able to switch much of its goods traffic to the much faster route. Passenger services were considerably improved from 1936 by the introduction of what were known as the Wairarapa railcars, which cut an hour off the Wellington-Masterton journey, most of the time-saving coming from the elimination of shunting at Summit and Cross Creek. These railcars could climb the incline under their own power but did have a centre-rail brake for descents. There was also a combination passenger-parcel railcar service that took Cross Creek children to secondary school in

Masterton; on the return journey it dropped off groceries, supplies and parcels loaded at Masterton.

In 1948 it was decided that a tunnel needed to be built. The Rimutaka tunnel was opened to traffic on 3 November 1955. The incline was consigned to history and now, without its rails or the screeching whistles of the Fell locomotives, is open to the public as part of the Rimutaka Forest Park. The world's last remaining Fell engine is on display at Featherston.

Main North Line (Addington–Picton)

Length: 348.04 km.
Opened: 15 December 1945.
Passenger traffic: Daily Coastal Pacific between Picton and Christchurch.
Status: Open.

When the final section of the Christchurch-Picton section was opened for traffic in 1945 it was the culmination of a seventy-five year effort to link both ends of the South Island. By 1882 the 30 km Picton-Blenheim section had already been opened. The following year, when a royal commission tabled its report after investigating the line proposal, the recommendation was that no line should be built at that stage.

The Picton-Blenheim section had been opened to traffic on 18 November 1875. It was equipped with two small C class locomotives, seven passenger carriages and a variety of four-wheeler goods wagons. And, for twenty-five years, that was that: the 28.5 km rail connection between the two Marlborough towns operated as a self-contained isolated section with a morning train from Picton to Blenheim, returning in the afternoon. While a 4 km extension to Riverlands had opened in 1893, it was not until 1902, by which time the rails had reached Seddon, that any additional significant traffic was added. In 1911 the rails reached Ward, and in 1915 went on to Wharanui—a total length of 90.55 km but it was to be another twenty-five years before trains could go any further southward. In 1936 the work gangs began to lay track beyond Wharanui, with the line being opened to Clarence in October 1942, and thereupon a Picton-Clarence passenger service began. Two years later the Picton section reached its greatest length with the extension to Kaikoura, making 157.5 km in all.

Then came the depression of the late 1880s, which deepened in the early 1890s. In the first decade of the twentieth century the railheads of what would become the Main North line moved closer together: by 1915 the line from Christchurch was open as far as Parnassus. And there matters stood until 1925, when NZR looked at the feasibility of a rail ferry service between Wellington and Picton. It concluded the potential traffic was insufficient to justify either the shipping service or the completion of the line.

Another four years passed until Public Works Minister Ethelbert Ransom announced formation work was under way north of Parnassus, but this burst of activity lasted only until 1931 due to government spending cuts as the latest depression took hold. The election of the Labour Government in 1935 saw the project revived and another 50 km built, the new railheads being Hundalee (1939) and Clarence. In 1944 traffic was operating southwards from Picton as far as Kaikoura, the gap between Kaikoura and Hundalee being closed in 1945. Railcars were introduced in 1956, running between Christchurch and Picton.

The Main North line received a boost in traffic from August 1962 when the first roll-on, roll-off ferry — the *Aramoana* — came into service between Wellington and Picton. The rail-equipped ferry meant the end of mixed trains on the line: locomotives were kept fully occupied hauling all the freight wagons that came and went across Cook Strait on the new ferry; there was no traction capacity for pulling heavy passenger carriages.

Hundalee, once having had the relative importance of being a railhead, disappeared from railway timetables in 1982 when the station was closed to all traffic. Other stations on the line closed by 1985 included Parnassus, Domett and Ethelton, although the unattended stations of Scargill and Mina were still on the express timetable as 'stopping if required' stations.

Midland Line

Length: 211.27 km.
Opened: 4 August 1923 on completion of the Otira tunnel. Otira tunnel electrified 1923-1998.
Passenger services: operated by daily TranzAlpine service.

This line, which links Christchurch with Greymouth and pierces the Southern Alps, was certainly one of the most daunting rail engineering challenges in New Zealand and was initially to have been built by a private company. That the company involved failed was not a surprise given the scale of the task involved; but perhaps that it failed so soon in its life might not have been expected.

Railway building on the Canterbury side of the mountain range was no picnic either. In the end, the section between Springfield and Arthur's Pass required sixteen tunnels, five viaducts including the 73-metre-high Staircase, the 55-metre high Broken River and the 39-metre high Slovens Creek viaducts, along with several substantial bridges. Arthur's Pass, 737 metres above sea level, was opened to traffic on 1 July 1914. Thus there remained a gap between that settlement and Otira on the other side of the mountains. In the meantime, horse-drawn coaches traversed the high road between the two railheads.

Many options were considered for crossing the Southern Alps: switchbacks, spiral tunnels, winding-engines to pull trains up steep grades or a rack (or Fell) system similar to that over the Rimutaka Ranges, together with the prospect of a summit tunnel — all these were actively considered. In the end, a tunnel through the mountain range itself was the only practicable solution. The government in 1908 accepted a tender of just under £600,000 and work began. It would be thirteen years before the tunnel was completed.

The Midland Line today but memories of yesteryear evoked as restored 4-6-2 Ab 663 pauses at Cass with its excursion. This locomotive, now owned by Mainline Steam of Auckland, in 1920 hauled the royal train when used by the Prince of Wales (later King Edward VIII and then the Duke of Windsor). (*Roy Sinclair*)

High rainfall, snow, ice and difficult rock formation all took their toll of the contractor, J. H. McLean & Sons. In 1912, the year scheduled for completion of the tunnel, the government took over this project with only about a third of the work having been completed. The breach between the two ends took place in August 1918, but another four and a half years passed before the job was finished. At 8,554 metres in length, and at the time the longest tunnel in the Southern Hemisphere, the track dropped at an average gradient of 1 in 33 from the Arthur's Pass end. The more important consideration was that, in other direction, trains had to battle a rising 1 in 33 gradient and, for this reason, electric traction was considered the only feasible way to move trains up such a sleep gradient. This issue was doubly important because most of the traffic on the line—timber and then coal—moves west to east, against the grade.

Initially, the line earned considerable revenue from timber being hauled out of Westland and from coal being railed for use in various parts of the South Island. But the forests were depleted and your average South Island home is no longer heated by coal fires nor the evening meal cooked on a coal range. In the other direction, the small population on West Coast limited the freight task for trains travelling westward. The line stays in operation mainly to service the coal traffic from the West Coast transported to ships at Lyttelton, Christchurch's port.

One of the more important stations along the line was Springfield, located on the western edge of the Canterbury Plains and at the start of the steeper grades as the line climbs towards the Southern Alps. It was a railhead for twenty-six years; it was not until 29 October 1906 that trains were able to push further westwards to the new railhead at Staircase. In the latter years of the steam era, smaller locomotives continued to haul trains from Christchurch but at Springfield the powerful Kb engines were attached for the 1-in-50 grades on the way to Arthur's Pass. As late as the 1950s it was usual for at least nine locomotive crews to be stationed at Springfield. The station was equipped with refreshment rooms. The station was not a large generator of freight traffic; the settlement was located at the very edge of the wheat-growing areas of the Canterbury Plains. In 1890, for example, less than 500 tons of wheat was consigned from Springfield. Apart from the sale of passenger tickets, Springfield's main business was the handling of sheep for transport by rail.

In 1997 new ventilation systems were installed in the Otira tunnel so that diesel-electric locomotives could be used to haul coal trains up the steep grade, thus making redundant the old, less powerful Eo electric engines. The ventilation can cope with four DX diesels on a train. Water sprays were also installed where the coal trains enter the tunnel, ensuring no coal dust problems while underground.

Main South Line (Lyttelton-Invercargill)
(Also referred to as the South Island Main Trunk)

Length: 601.4 krn.
Opened: 22 January 1879. Electrified Lyttelton-Christchurch 1929-1970.
Passenger services: Lyttelton-Christchurch closed to passengers 28 February 1972. Southerner between Christchurch and Invercargill withdrawn February 2002.

With the completion of the Balclutha to Clinton section of this line in 1879, through running between three main cities of the South Island was at last made possible. The first express train between Invercargill and Dunedin, a Yankee K class locomotive hauling a rake of six-wheeler carriages, ran on 22 January 1879, taking six hours and a half hours for the journey. Henceforth it became possible to travel between Christchurch and Invercargill in two days with an overnight stop in Dunedin.

The Main South, or South Island Main Trunk as it was often called, had its genesis in several isolated sections built by or at the behest of provincial governments: Lyttelton-Christchurch-Rakaia (Canterbury). Dunedin-Port Chalmers (Otago) and Bluff-Invercargill (Southland). Before the completion of the Lyttelton tunnel on 9 November 1867, the Canterbury authorities adopted the interim measure of a line out to Ferrymead on the Heathcote River where boats plied to and from the province's main port. On 1 December 1863 the first passenger train left the original Christchurch station site for Ferrymead.

Extensions from Rakaia (which was served by the provincial broad gauge) began in 1873, with trains running to Ashburton from 24 August 1874 (the line would be converted to narrow gauge over the next two years). Meanwhile gangs were working northwards from Timaru, with the line open as far as Temuka by 26 October 1875. The intermediate section required some expensive bridge construction. The Rakaia had already been crossed with what was—and remains—New Zealand's longest bridge at 1,744 metres, but other wide rivers had to be bridged on the Canterbury Plains, with the Rangitata North bridge at Ealing at 610 metres long being the other main obstacle to overcome. The rail builders had already crossed the Opihi River near Temuka with a 504-metre-long bridge while the rails between Waitaki and Glenavy required New Zealand's second longest rail bridge to be constructed, the 914-metre structure over the Waitaki River.

Kb 968 waits on the main line while Ja 1266 moves into the loop at Winchester in South Canterbury. In 1939 NZR built six heavy 4-8-4 Kb locomotives to work on the Midland line, mainly on the section beyond Springfield where the track climbs into the foothills of the Southern Alps. On the day of this photograph, however, the Kb is working the Main South line on 27 February 1969, a balmy summer afternoon and in the final year of the Kb's life. After that, the Ja class had only two more years to go. Then this water vat would be demolished and eventually the four-wheel wagon would be phased out. (*Wilson Lythgoe*)

The hardest work was building the line northwards of Sawyers Bay on what was until then the Dunedin-Port Chalmers line. The section between there and Waitati remains one of the most breathtaking on the New Zealand system as the trains edge their way up the gradient from Otago Harbour, through the 1,408 metre Mihiwhaka tunnel and then past the now closed little stations of The Gums, Osborne and Cliffs, always with panoramic views of the coastline and Pacific Ocean.

Little by little the gaps were closing. The line reached Oamaru in February 1877 and the following year there was through running to Dunedin. In the other direction, Dunedin-Balclutha running was possible once the 437-metre steel bridge over the Clutha River was finished. All that remained was the 34 km gap between Clinton and Balclutha, that being closed with the driving of the last spike in January 1879. The link between the South Island's three main towns was now complete: travellers from the North Island could step off the overnight ferry from Wellington once it berthed at Lyttelton and then make their way by rail to Christchurch, Dunedin or Invercargill.

However, it was not until 1 November 1904 that a one-train through service was established between Christchurch and Invercargill. From 1904 the Christchurch-Invercargill service took 14hr 40min. In 1949 the Limited expresses were introduced on the run for three days a week (the standard expresses ran the other days, and stopping at the smaller stations) reducing the journey to 11hr 20min.

In 1970 the Main South entered the modern rail era with the introduction of the Southerner service. This train represented a sea change in NZR attitudes toward passengers and was the first serious effort in decades to win travellers back to rail. The Southerner was a new concept in New Zealand: a train serving only the main stations with buses running in parallel serving the smaller stations now no longer on the express time-table (Temuka and Rakaia being two examples), and connecting with the train at the main stations. At the beginning of the new service NZR had been rigorous in eliminating the smaller intermediate stations from the Southerner timetable; stops were made at only Gore, Balclutha, Dunedin, Oamaru, Timaru and Ashburton. Gradually, local campaigns got several stops restored to the timetable on a 'stops if required' basis: thus Edendale, Mataura, Milton, Mosgiel and Palmerston were back.

Initially the train's buffet cars offered hot meals (eventually reduced to snacks) while hostesses served alcoholic and other drinks to passengers seated in smoking cars, leaving the non-smoking carriages alcohol-free. Southerner meals were the first served on NZR trains since the demise of the dining cars in 1917.

Alas, the Southerner's introduction coincided with declining rail patronage as car ownership grew and bus services provided opposition. Even in holiday seasons the train was down to just three carriages compared with six or more in the 1980s. In 2001 no buyer could be found to take over running the train and the passenger service closed in February 2002.

* * *

4

Stations — Great and Small

It may have boasted the country's longest railway station name — Lake Omapere Road Crossing — but by 1973 the structure itself  was hardly a tribute to the NZR's maintenance programme. The station was located on the Okaihau branch in the country's far north; it was the second most northerly station in New Zealand, the terminus at Okaihau being the northernmost. Notwithstanding the state of the station, a passenger service in the form of a carriage at the end of a goods train was still passing here and would surivive for another three years. (*Wilson Lythgoe*).

THE LONGEST STATION NAME on the New Zealand system was given to northernmost but one, Lake Omapere Road Crossing on the Okaihau branch. Four stations tied for the shortest: Ava (a passenger stop on the Wellington-Upper Hutt suburban service), Kew (on the Bluff branch from Invercargill), Oio (on the North Island Main Trunk) and Tui (on the Nelson section).

Other station curiosities included Kaiwharawhara which, notwithstanding having four platforms and dozens of trains stopping there each day, never had a station building (shelters only) or staff. Summit station at the top of the former Rimutaka Incline had a signal box but no station building or platform (passengers stayed in the carriages while the train was pulled apart and then reassembled as the Fell locomotives were placed along the consist for the Incline climb or descent).

Paeroa may have been the third most-used name on the NZR system: over the years there was Paeroa, Paeroa Township and Paeroa South.

The second-most frequently used name, or part of a name, was 'Racecourse'. Racecourse Platform served Auckland's Ellerslie's course; there was Waverley Racecourse on the New Plymouth line; Park Racecourse was a stop on the old Gisborne section (later the Moutohora branch); Te Rapa Racecourse Platform served Hamilton's racecourse; also used by trains were Hastings Racecourse, Foxton Racecourse, Gore Racecourse, Wyndham Racecourse (on the Glenham branch) and others over the years. Hornby in the Christchurch area was first called Racecourse; there was also a stopping place of that name outside Timaru's racing venue. Riverton Racecourse was located on the Tuatapere branch in Southland. The Gracefield branch (running off the Wellington-Upper Hutt suburban line) had a station called Hutt Park, race trains being the only passenger services to use the industrial line (serving, among others, the NZR Hutt railway workshops and various oil company sidings) that ran past the racecourse of that name.

The Maori prefix 'Te' was used on thirty-two stations, from Te Akeake on the Opua line in Northland to Te Wharau on the Dargaville branch. In 1936, NZR published a small booklet with translation of Maori station names. Among them:

North Island

Kaitoke — Cold food
Okahukura — The place of the rainbow
Paekakariki — Wooden perch for green parakeet
Paeroa — Long ridge
Papakura — Level land of red soil
Rotorua —Two lakes
Taneatua — Tane the God
Taumarunui — Place of abundant shade
Tauranga — The resting place
Te Awamutu — The river end

South Island

Hokitika — To return in a straight line (as in sea navigation)
Inangahua — Preserved whitebait
Ngawakau — The shags
Oamaru — Sacred food for god Maru
Otira — Food for a journey
Rangiora — Day of health
Tokarahi —Dead rock
Waimate — Dead water

As noted earlier, NZR once operated 1,350 railway stations. Even in 1973, after many branches had been closed, there were still 760 stations designated as being open to traffic. A report that year advised the government that stations should be closed immediately if they were not turning over revenue of $70,000 a year. That would have struck off 650 stations at one blow. The advice was not followed and the closures were drawn out over the years.

Few of the hundreds of wooden railway stations that once existed in New Zealand survive, so this equivalent of an NZR Class 4 station would be valuable in itself. But it doubly interesting because it is the only remaining structure built by the Wellington and Manawatu Railway Company. The station has been enlarged three times: in 1902 there was added a parcels/luggage room; in 1910 it got a verandah; and in 1936 a larger parcels/luggage room was built. The station is still used by passengers, it being a stopping place for the daily return Capital Connection between Palmerston North and Wellington. (*Horowhenua Historical Trust Inc.*)

Pelichet Bay was probably the first station to succumb to the growth of road transport. The station was located about one kilometre north of Dunedin. It was closed in 1925 because the land on which it stood was needed for a new road to allow access to the New Zealand and South Seas Exhibition in Dunedin and the main railway line was shifted away from this small station. It was not only the competition from road lorries that doomed lines: many lost their purpose if the main customer went out of business. Maharahara on the Hawke's Bay line had taken a blow when the local dairy factory closed in the early 1950s but it struggled on until fertiliser traffic was moved to a station further along the line. Maharahara was closed to all traffic on 30 March 1975. While the 1930s through the 1950s were typified by many wayside stations losing their passenger services, in later years many stations in suburban areas lost their goods yards as industries closed or switched to road transport. This writer recalls unloading four-wheel wagons at sidings at Naenae station while working during school holidays for a nearby wool and hide business. Petone and Lower Hutt were busy goods stations, Petone have a network of sidings, including one where cars produced by the adjacent Austin car plant were loaded for distribution around New Zealand. All these yards have gone but the stations concerned, of course, have thrived as parts of the Wellington suburban commuter train system.

A tourist train service has saved this station. The Dunedin Railways tourist service runs a daily train from Dunedin through the spectacular Taieri Gorge as far as Pukerangi, where the engine runs around the train for the return journey. (*Dunedin Railways*)

Auckland

Auckland at last has a station in its downtown area. A suburban working awaits departure from Britomart station. (*Roy Sinclair*)

The history of Auckland's railway stations has not been an entirely happy one. Between 1930 and 2003 New Zealand's largest city was without a rail terminus close to the central business district.

The city's first station was opened at Britomart Point on 24 December 1863, to serve trains running on the new line between Auckland and Onehunga. Auckland's second station, Queen Street, was opened just behind the old Chief Post Office in 1885 — behind being the operative word. So, while the station was located in the centre of the city, it was hidden behind the post office and thus not visually a part of everyday life in

Auckland. Gradually, as the rails spread out from Auckland, this station was used by an increasing number of important trains: the Main Trunk expresses (from 1909), the Opua Express in 1923 and the Taneatua Express in 1928.

The decision to move the station site to outside the central business district in 1930 was, in retrospect, widely regarded as a disaster, in that it consigned the railway to a secondary place in Auckland's transport scene. While a grand structure, the new site was doomed to be an unsuccessful development because the planned mid-city loop to the northern line was never built. By the late 1940s use of this huge station with its six platforms was dwindling, due to the coal shortages that saw passenger services curtailed throughout New Zealand. Auckland did not have the level of suburban services that continued to make Wellington station such thriving operation, but it did see some increases in passenger traffic with the introduction in 1956 of railcar services to Northland and New Plymouth, and in 1959 to Te Puke and Rotorua. Then there were daylight Blue Streak railcars running between Auckland and Wellington from 1968 and the introduction of the all-sleeper Silver Star in 1971. At Auckland, NZR adopted the system common on many overseas railways of collecting tickets at the exit gate from suburban trains and inspecting long distance tickets as passengers arrived at the platform.

Throughout the 1990s it was hoped that rails could be brought back into the centre of Auckland by the construction of a line, including a 506-metre tunnel, to the Britomart site. In 1999 the Auckland City Council voted against going ahead with the Britomart project. Nevertheless, the work on the cut-and-cover tunnel continued with the council promising that it was still the intention to bring rails underground to a new station near the old Chief Post Office — and thus bringing the story of Auckland's railway stations full circle.

In 2000 Auckland City Council announced it would build a new downtown transport centre. In 2003 Britomart opened — this time not hidden behind the by then unused Chief Post Office, the project instead using the (by theh unused) post office as the frontage for the terminal.

Wellington

The southern terminus of the North Island's railway system, Wellington is the busiest passenger station in New Zealand. The first station was located at Pipitea Point, a small promontory in Wellington Harbour later included in the reclamations for the Quay complex of wharves. The station opened in 1874 when rail services began between Wellington and the Hutt Valley (but was destroyed by fire in 1878). The government system thereupon built Lambton station in 1880 by which time rail services had reached as far as the Wairarapa.

The Wellington and Manawatu Railway Company, when formed, favoured the idea of a combined Wellington terminal with NZR, but agreement was not reached and so the company built its own station (Thorndon) opened in November 18866. This was taken over by NZR in 1908 when the government bought out the company, and a year later NZR was using Thorndon for its express services.

NZR in the 1930s decided that a whole new station complex was needed in Wellington, and the present building was
opened on 19 June 1937.

An eighty-eight seater accelerates out of one on Wellington's
passenger platforms at the beginning of a daily service to one of
the various provincial destinations operated out of the capital.
The lines behind the railcar were used to stable carriages used
only in mornings and late afternoons to augment the electric
multiple unit peak hour services to and from Taita in the Hutt
Valley. (*Bob Stott*)

With its nine platforms, the new terminus was an immediate
success, and was seeing trains arrive and depart every five minutes at peak hours. (There could be as many as 140 movements
a day.) Express trains pulled out of Wellington for Auckland,

New Plymouth and Napier, and later there would be railcar services to many provincial centres in the lower North Island. The new station also housed the NZR Head Office, occupying 230 rooms in total. The concourse level included a dining room as well as a cafeteria, baths, bookstall, fruit stall, post office and a men's barbershop. It is now a listed building.

Also in the early 1930s, a large area of the harbour was reclaimed for new new railway yards, a development which also created Aotea Quay and its string of wharves serving overseas cargo and passenger ships. In addition to the large marshalling yard just 'across the road' from one of New Zealand's main ports, there was a network of carriage sidings where suburban consists were stabled for peak-hour operations. But by the 1990s it was becoming clear that Wellington's yards needed to be redesigned, For one thing, the freight arrival and departure roads were too short to accommodate modern train lengths; these roads were between 400 metres long, whereas the new era trains could be up to 750 metres. The redesign coincided with the construction of a new stadium on part of what had been railway marshalling yards.

Christchurch

The South Island's largest city has had three railway locations. The first station, built by Canterbury Provincial Council, served the broad gauge line to Ferrymead. In 1877 the station site was moved to Moorhouse Avenue at one end of Colombo Street; at the other was Cathedral Square and the centre of the city. This second station was once a hive of activity. There were boat trains arriving from the steamer wharf at Lyttelton (ferries ran overnight between there and Wellington in each direction); the station's refreshment rooms offered a sit-down full breakfast for hungry travellers from the ship before they caught their onward express trains.

By 1923 and the opening of the Otira tunnel through the Southern Alps the station roster grew to accommodate express trains running to and from the West Coast. Then in 1945, with the completion of the line north to Picton, there were added the long distance passenger services on the Main North line. Christchurch was also the base for passenger services running out to the Southbridge and Little River branch lines; there were also passenger services using mixed trains leaving for Springfield on the Midland line and suburban trains operating to Lyttelton (until 1972) and Rangiora (until 1976). Night expresses ran to and from Dunedin (and were maintained by railcars into the 1970s).

This second station was in 1960 replaced on the same site by a modernist brick structure, although its vast size was out of keeping with the decline in passenger traffic.

In 1993 a new station was built across from the site of the former Addington workshops and now serves the long distance tourist train services to the West Coast and Picton.

Five years later all freight handling in Christchurch was brought together on one site with the opening of the Middleton freight terminal. Since the 1930s, NZR goods train operating into and out of Christchurch required considerable shunting operations due to the widely-spaced locations of the freight yards — the old shed near the original station had been 3.5 km from Middleton, with the Waltham freight shed located even farther away on the Lyttelton line. Even until the 1990s, wagons had to be shunted back and forth between these two yards. Middleton had first been used for assembling goods trains in 1927 but this was closed during the Great Depression, only to be reopened in 1946 with nineteen sidings with incoming trains broken up and outgoing ones assembled.

Greymouth

Until 1923 Greymouth was the centre of an isolated NZR system, with rails going south to Hokitika and Ross, and inland and northwards to Westport and Seddonville. In addition, trains operated out of Greymouth to the Rewanui, Rapahoe and Blackball branches. Most traffic — and most traffic was coal — came into Greymouth to be loaded aboard colliers for transport to other parts of the Dominion. Greymouth's hopes of being linked to Nelson had faded by 1923 but a new railway era was about to launched with the opening of the Otira tunnel and a rail connection with the east coast of the South Island.

Such was the scope of traffic worked in and out of Greymouth that a sizeable fleet of locomotives was stationed there. To accommodate them, NZR constructed what was considered one of the more notable railway landmarks in New Zealand: the Elmer Lane roundhouse, a magnificent steam locomotive depot unmatched by any depot on the NZR system (there was another roundhouse, at Invercargill, but it was smaller).

Greymouth has one of the few historic stations remaining on the New Zealand railway system, its survival due largely to the popularity of the TranzAlpine passenger service from Christchurch. The building was given a facelift in 1997 ahead of its centenary that year. Restoration architects were consulted to ensure that Greymouth retained its heritage values befitting a Class Two NZR station.

Oamaru

This station was unusual in that its original location required all through trains to reverse out of it. The first station was located on what was essentially a spur line. An express from Christchurch, for example, would pull into the platform and then the locomotive would run around the train, be attached at the other end and then run back to the main line, this time the points being set to set the train in the direction of Dunedin. The station's location was due to the fact that Oamaru had initially been at one end of an isolated section. The section south to Dunedin was begun later.

Not much detail remains of the original station, but in 1896 the Oamaru Mail published a letter from an irate traveller complaining about the state of it.

> Every time a train was drawn up to the platform the crowd surged up and down in an endeavour to secure a seat, and often when they got it they found they were on the wrong train. Women and children were pushed and hustled about in a most disgraceful manner. It was a splendid opportunity for the light-fingered gentry, and one that was taken full advantage of. Several persons, chiefly ladies, had their pockets picked, one having her purse taken, the money extracted, and the empty purse replaced.

A new station was built in 1900, this time on the main line. It had a large dining room which could seat 250 people for lunch when the expresses made their twenty-four minute stop (in the postwar years, two shillings and sixpence would get you soup, a main course (roast sirloin of beef with Yorkshire pudding being a staple on the menu) and a sweet pudding, usually involving either custard or jelly. There was a kiosk where you could buy newspaper, magazines and comic books or hire a pillow for the remainder of the journey.

Oamaru was once the terminus for services on three branch lines — those on the Tokarahi, Ngapara and Kurow lines. The first was closed in 1930, the second (apart from a short section to a lime works) in 1959 and the third in 1983. In the 1960s, Oamaru was a very busy place with cement being shipped through up the Kurow line for the construction on the Aviemore and Benore hydroelectric stations.

Dunedin

Dunedin station has the longest platform in New Zealand at 900 metres. In the heyday of rail travel, trains could be so long that they spilled out beyond both the end of the platform and and the departure signals. The station also had dock platforms at each end — at the north, used by Port Chalmers suburban services among others; at the southern end, by Mosgiel and Central Otago passenger trains.

The present station is the third in Dunedin. The first (1872-1875) was built for the Dunedin and Port Chalmers Railway Company. It was replaced in 1875 with a new government station. The third (and existing) structure was designed by architect Sir George Troup. Stone was bought from Hyde in Central Otago for the main body of the station, with Oamaru limestone used for the facings and ornamental work. The foundation stone was laid by the then Minister of Railways, Joseph Ward, on 3 June 1904. The station was completed in November 1907, the total cost coming to £120,000, a massive sum for its time (by which time Ward had become Prime Minister). Apart from the magnificent exterior, including a thirty-seven metre-high dock tower, the station was known for the mosaic floor in the entrance hall; made by Royal Doulton and made with 725,760 porcelain tiles together depicting railway scenes and carrying carrying NZR's logo. This floor was replaced with a replica in the 1960s.

Sunday at Dunedin as Vulcan railcar RM 56 accelerates away from New Zealand's longest railway platform and heads off to Alexandra on the Otago Central line; up until 1958, these railcars had run all the way to Cromwell, the terminus of that line. Meanwhile Ja 1264 has just collected a roadsider van from the dock platform line and will attach it to the Sunday-only Dunedin-Invercargill express, the next train to depart Dunedin from the main platform. Note the profusion of rolling stock in the sidings behind the railcar — those carriages and wagons, and the sidings themselves, all long gone. (*Wilson Lythgoe*)

Until the late 1960s Dunedin station was a very busy place. Some of the passenger services — such as the morning and afternoon country trains to and from Oamaru and Clinton, or the holiday expresses to Cromwell — had disappeared or were in their last years, but there were still suburban services to Port Chalmers and Mosgiel, railcars to and from Christchurch, Invercargill, Palmerston and Alexandra and — of course — the Christchurch-Invercargill expresses (as well as the Friday and Sunday night passenger services to Christchurch). Before the demise of the suburban trains, about 4,000 people a daily caught or alighted from trains at the station. However, with the demise of the two daily Southerner trains, the station's sole use now is as the base for excursion trains operated by the Dunedin Railways tourist rail operation.

In 1993 substantial track alterations were made at Dunedin to allow the sale of the some of the land. Overall, trackage within the yards shrank from 12 km to 4 km in total length. That year also saw the sale of the station building to the Dunedin City Council. In 2000 a $4 million restoration project concluded after several years of work.

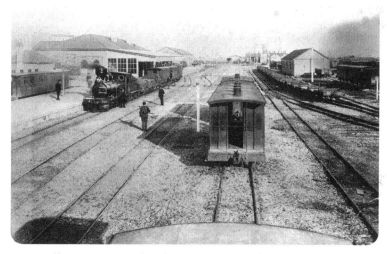

Invercargill was not only the terminus of the Main South line, but was also the originating station for trains travelling on five branch lines: Bluff, Seaward Bush to Tokanui, Tuatapere, Mossburn and Kingston. This photograph, taken in the railway's first decades, post-dates the structure built by the Southland Provincial Council for its original 1,435 mm gauge line, that first station having an awning extending over the main passenger line. This photograph was taken long after the government took over the line and converted it to 1,067 mm gauge track. This photo shows station staff posing as a J class locomotive prepares to leave with a mixed train. (*Southland Museum and Art Gallery*)

Visual pollution was not a consideration in 1912. Lumsden's goods shed is plastered with advertisements aimed at people waiting on the platform or sitting on the trains. Passenger services operated out of Lumsden on the Kingston branch (Invercargill-Kingston) or the two other lines that were served out of this station — the Waimea Plains line to Gore or the short Mossburn branch. (*Southland Museum and Art Gallery*)

* * *

5

They Ran the Trains

THE ORIGINAL GOVERNMENT RAILWAY authority in New Zealand was established with the passing of the Immigration and Public Works Act 1870. This legislation gave the central government the authority to decide which railway projects should be approved in conjunction with the provincial councils. All railways came under the control of the Public Works Act as of 1 November 1876, the day upon which provincial councils ceased to exist. The department inherited the provincial-built lines, comprising three different railway systems — those built by provincial councils in Canterbury, Otago and Southland (all in the South Island). The new administration introduced uniform operations and ordered that all lines be converted to the national 1,067 mm narrow gauge.

Before 1870, three provinces had had announced plans to build lines (Auckland, Canterbury and Southland) while Otago authorised a privately owned railway. Otago even set up its own railway department to oversee the Dunedin & Port Chalmers Railway Company, which ran trains between Dunedin and its nearest port. Auckland's provincial council spent almost £100,000 and achieved little more than a few miles of formation work. None of the other provinces had the financial ability to undertake such projects and, indeed, Southland Provincial Council's efforts in railway construction contributed in a considerable way to that council's eventual bankruptcy. Southland built two lines to the 1,485 mm gauge, including one 12.8 km section using wooden rails to save money.

Even after a railway department was established in 1880, the Public Works Department (PWD) continued to oversee the construction of lines; typically, it would build a line complete with stations and goods sheds and then hand over operations to New Zealand Railways. Often lines were opened in sections with initial freight and even passenger trains run by the PWD.

I

The New Zealand Government Railways Department, almost always referred to as NZR, was established in 1880 but reported to the Minister for Public Works, not getting its own minister (Alfred Jerome Cadman) until 1895. Such was the importance of railways on the New Zealand political scene that three Prime Ministers held the railways portfolio at the same time as leading the government — William Massey (1919-1922), Gordon Coates (1925-1928) and George Forbes (1931-1935).

The New Zealand Railways Corporation was established in 1982 to take over the work of the department, the government believing there was a need to reorganise a network it saw as hopelessly overstaffed and inefficient.

Then in 1990 a subsequent government decided to corporatise the railways, writing off $1.2 billion of debt and injecting $360 million in new capital. In 1993 the railway system was sold to a private company, Tranz Rail, for $328.3 million. Tranz Rail was a consortium of financial companies and United States rail operator Wisconsin Central. The private owner built new locomotives and focused on long-haul express freight services. Many long-distance passenger services were scrapped: the Bay Express (Wellington-Napier), the Waikato Connection (Auckland-Hamilton), the Southerner (Christchurch-Invercargill), the Geyserland Express (Auckland-Rotorua), the Kaimai Express (Auckland-Tauranga) and the Northerner (Auckland-Wellington overnight service).

Then in 2003 the New Zealand railway operation came under the control of an Australian transport group, Toll Holdings. It tired of the business and sold out to the Labour government in 2008 for $665 million, the government establishing KiwiRail as the state-owned operator. The Auckland suburban system is now operated a subsidiary of the French group Veolia.

And then there were the private operators of an earlier era, none of which lasted all that long.

Castlecliff Railway Company

Length: 5.58 km
Opened: 31 October 1885
Passenger services: Ended October 1932
Status: Sold to NZR on 1 February 1956 — thus removing the last privately owned railway company in New Zealand, a

situation which existed until the privatisationo of the network in the 1990s.

This line was built by the Wanganui Head Railway Company, which in 1889 became the Castlecliff Railway Company after the original operators encountered economic difficulties and financial reconstruction was required. The company was formed to fill the gap between the terminus of the NZR's Wanganui branch and the town's port. On 4 August 1884 a crowd turned out by the twin's gas works to witness the turning of the first sod. Chairman George Hutchison told the assembly that the project had survived difficulties and opposition on every side. According to the Wanganui Herald, Hutchison added that 'the beginning of their enterprise was strangely associated with a beginning of depression all over New Zealand and I think this is a happy augury that the dark cloud of depression which seems to be all over the land is now breaking'. After the turning of the sod, 'those present, at the invitation of the directors, drank success to the Heads Railway Company in bumpers of champagne'.

The agreement with the government was that NZR would provide labour, clerical assistance, stores, stationery and tools and charge accordingly. It went on:

> Upon twenty-four hours' notice in writing from the company the Minister will supply a locomotive complete, with labour and stores, at per day of eight working hours or part thereof, £4, when specially put into steam for the company. If at any time the company should ask for the use of an engine not put into steam specially for the company, if the Minister be able to supply it, he will do so at a charge of

£1 per return trip. The Minister will supply carriage-stock at such times as it may be convenient to the Railway Department — only when so supplied, the following charges will be made at one day or part thereof: First-class, six-wheeled carriage, 10s; composite or second-class carriage, 7s 6d; first-class small carriage, 6s; composite or second-class carriage, 4s; brake-van, 3s ... Terminal charges will be made by the Minister to the company as follows: For each passenger starting from or arriving at Wanganui the company shall pay the Minister 1d., and for each parcel despatched from or arriving at Wanganui the company shall pay the Minister 1d per cwt* or part of a hundredweight.

(* A hundredweight, or cwt, was a unit of 112 pounds, or 50.8 kg.)

Initially the passenger services were popular. In 1913 we see advertisements promoting the railway as a mode for those wanting to fish, picnic or sea bathe. Seven return services ran each weekday (starting at 6.10 am and finishing at 5.35 pm, with an evening train on Saturdays. Five return services operated on Sundays. But the line, so far as passengers were concerned, fought a losing battle when electric tram services began in Wanganui.

The Castlecliff company operated small tank locomotives, the best known being named Moana and Belmont. In 1972, Cecil H. V. Steere, writing in Rails magazine, recalled the time when before the introduction in 1917 of six o'clock closing of all bars as a 'temporary' wartime measure—it would last until 1967—when 'either Belmont or Moana waited until the pubs shut at ten o'clock before the last passenger train left for Castlecliff. Sympathetic train crews usually delayed their (10.00 pm) departure until the last stragglers had climbed unsteadily aboard the old-fashioned four-wheel wooden cars'.

By 1932 passenger traffic had become uneconomic and the company instead concentrated on its freight business, helped by the growth of new industries in Wanganui and the increasing phosphate shipments from Nauru and Ocean Island. In 1953 the Wanganui Harbour Board made representations to the then Railways Commission asking that the small railroad which had served the district for so many years be taken over by the government. As Steere recounts, 'less than three years later the four mile line from Wanganui to the Heads became part of the national system. The shrill whistles of Moana, Belmont and other veteran locomotives had been heard for the last time'.

Duntroon and Hakataramea Railway Company

This company built what would be known as the Kurow branch which left the Main South at Pukeuri, just north of Oamara, ran inland roughly parallel with the Waitaki River as far as Kurow, then turned right and ran over a bridge across the Waitaki River to the tiny settlement of Hakataramea, a distance of 60.3 km. The Duntroon and Hakataramea Railway Company was formed with capital of £150,000 put by local identities including Robert Campbell, a member of the Legislative Council and former Oamaru member of the House of Representatives. It let a contract for building the line and work began in 1879. The line was handed over to the government in 1885.

Hutt Park Railway Company

Length: 3.1 km
Opened: 1885
Passenger services: Race trains operated on this line
Status: Closed 1983

The Hutt Park Railway Company built a line, opened in 1885, which left the Wellington-Hutt railway just south of the existing Petone yards and for 3.1 km along the foreshore of Wellington Harbour to Hutt Park station on the western side of the mouth of the Hutt River, close to the 'pipe bridge' (as it was always known to the locals because it carried water pipes). The line's construction was motivated by the desire to preserve the importance of the Hutt Park racecourse in the face of a plan to build another course at Island Bay in Wellington. The Hutt course had been declining in popularity because of the difficulty racegoers had getting there. Stewards of the racing club figured prominently among the promoters of the new company, which raised £4,000 in capital. One of the directors was Joseph Saunders, who had also invested in the Wellington and Manawatu Railway Company.

The railway was built in thirty-eight days by operating shifts of workers around the clock. The line stopped short of the Hutt River because the cost of building a rail bridge was prohibitive, so racegoers were required to walk from Hutt Park station across the pipe bridge. The terminus station had a ticket box and waiting room. Another station, Beach, was erected at the other end of the line, at the junction with the NZR rails.

NZR operated the line on behalf of the company although one account suggests that the company had its own steam locomotive to work goods traffic on the line. The company's plans at one time included the laying of a branch to the Petone gasworks and there was sporadic talk of a bridge across the river to allow the line to be extended to the racecourse.

In 1906 there was a proposal to build a wharf to serve Petone, with the Hutt Park line to provide the rail connection to the new jetty. However, NZR required the existing line be brought up to its standards (the tracks having suffered frequent damage from high seas) before NZR rolling stock could use it, but the company was not prepared to spend more money, the Wellington Racing Club having by this time moved to Trentham race course. The government refused to buy the railway and the new wharf was built without a rail connection. In 1908 the Gear Meat Company took control of the line and some time after 1915 lifted the track between its freezing works and the Hutt River, the line then ending just short of the settlers' memorial that dominates the Petone foreshore. In the 1950s it was a common sight for rakes of sheep wagons to be parked on the second road of the railway, having delivered their cargo to the works.

The Dominion, Wellington's morning newspaper, took the opportunity to recall the line's heyday on the day of the Hutt Park company's shareholders met to vote on winding up (24 November 1915) :

The race trains used to divert from the main line opposite the Marine Retreat Hotel and proceed slowly along the Hutt Park Railway Company's line, pulling up on a shingle track by the river. As soon as the train slowed it was a common sight to see hundreds of men dropping from the train and making a headlong dash to the pipe bridge. It was not just an ordinary kind of bridge, but just two or three planks floored over the Wainui water mains with wooden hand-rails, and only wide enough for the crowd to walk 'one abreast'. It was because it was such a slow business that the men used to rush, whilst the ladies, who had some respect for the race-day dresses, were wont to group up at the entrance of the bridge until the unchivalrous mob passed on.

Gear Meat operated what was classed as a siding until 1982 (rails also ran off it in the neighbouring Odlins timber yards) and the Esplanade line was lifted in 1983. Considering the economically tenuous nature of the original plan, it is astonishing that the line (at least, in part) survived for ninety-eight years.

The route of the line has disappeared under road widening.

Kaihu Valley Railway Company

The company took advantage of the Railway Construction and Land Act 1881 (which had been enacted primarily to assist the Wellington & Manawatu Railway Company — see below). The company was authorised to build a 26 km line in Northland province from the small port of Dargaville up the ; Valley in return for which the government granted it 5,870 hectares of land. But problems rose early in the company's history, primarily over survey parties being on Maori land. But considerable sums were raised: there were reports that between £40,000 and

£50,000 had been raised in Dunedin, then the financial capital of New Zealand (thanks to the wealth generated by the Central Otago gold rushes); in 1884 £50,000 was raised through debentures on the London market, the newspapers saying that £10,000 had by then already been spent building a large wharf at Dargaville and laying some track.

The line reached Opanake and was open to traffic from February 1889 and the company's timetable issued the following month showed trains operating in each direction each Tuesday and Friday with two return services on Saturdays. Trains left Dargaville at 8.15 am, stopping at Maitahi and Maropui, reaching Opanake at 9.25 am. The return service departed at 10.00 am. The trains were operated by a F class 0-6-0T which had been purchased by the company, although some accounts mention also a Dubs A class engine.

The company failed in 1890, with the government in May that year taking possession of the line to secure the £50,000 mortgage it had advanced. The government then tried unsuccessfully to find a buyer. The Public Works Department operated the line until the end of 1892, after which the track passed to NZR. That year, too, saw the winding up of the company; after £7,195 was repaid to the Colonial Bank and £435 to the liquidators, there was sufficient left to pay other creditors just one and a quarter pence in the pound. The shareholders lost everything.

The short extension was laid to Kaihu and by 1896 the line was profitable due to the growing haulage of the highly prized kauri timber. The railhead of Tarawhati was reached in

1914 and the construction ceased due to the war. The final leg to Donnelly's Crossing (35.91 km from Dargaville) was not opened to NZR trains until 1 April 1923 — forty-one years after work had first started. All stations on the line, including the grandly named Babylon, were, other than Dargaville, operated as unmanned flag stations. Passenger services were available throughout the life of the line in the form of a passenger car attached to goods trains.

The Kaihu railway remained an isolated section until 15 March 1943 when the NZR network finally reached Dargaville. However, the Kaihu line had begun losing money in the late 1920s as the forest resource was worked out, and the in 1930s local authorities began improving the roads. Such were the losses being recorded after the Second World War that the 1954 railways royal commission of that year recommend closure of the Kaihu line, that event taking effect on 19 July 1959.

Manawatu County Council

The Manawatu County Council owned and operated the Sanson Tramway between 25 August 1884 and 29 November 1945. The track formed a junction with the Foxton branch at Himitangi. The council took over the project after the failure in 1883 of the original promoter, the Foxton and Sanson Railway Company collapsed. The council decided to take up the project after a ratepayers' poll was decisively in favour

The tramway was about 22.5 km in length and played an important part in the opening up of the district, with the county council trains having running rights into Foxton along NZR tracks from Himitangi. Passengers and goods were carried; the county council made it clear it wanted to attract the widest variety of freight and nominated were horses, carriages, dogs, lambs, pigs, milk, rabbits and poultry, although wool and grain were expected to provide the greatest amount of revenue. The council's freight rates included a charge of one shilling per mile for corpses, although children's bodies were to be carried at half-price. A local blacksmith was contracted to look after repairs to the two locomotives.

There were several intermediate stopping places along the line, including Oroua Downs (where there was a cheese factory), Taikorea, Whale Line, Rosina, Rongotea Siding, Rowe's Siding (where there was a spur to Rowe's Flax Mill) and Penny's Siding. Motive power was provided by a succession of small locomotives, including one inherited from the Wellington and Manawatu Railway Company. The tramway's fate was part of a familiar story: first, the arrival of motor vehicles and, second, the decision by NZR not to allow its rolling stock on the tramway because of the poor state of the track (a problem which helped seal the fate of two other private lines, Hutt Park in Wellington and Ocean Beach in Dunedin).

For the Sanson Tramway, rearmament for the Second World War put off the inevitable. The construction of the Ohakea air base meant the tramway sprang back into life for the transport of construction materials, a task which put further wear on the track and the old rolling stock. The introduction of wartime petrol rationing saw the tramway once again used for general freight. As soon as the war was over, the tramway closed and was pulled up. In its last months all the general freight had gone back to road and the tramway's only task was carrying road metal. The council estimated the line would lose £500 a year, a fact which sealed the tramway's fate.

Midland Railway Company

The central government in 1887 enacted the Midland Railway Contract Act, which empowered the company of that name to build a 378 km line from Belgrove, where the government line from Nelson ended. Initially, the line would run to Brunner, near Greymouth, where it would . That completed, the company was then to take the rails across the Southern Alps to Springfield in Canterbury where, again, there was a terminus of a government line. It is conceivable that the company might have managed to build the first stage, although it involved some difficult country around Murchison, but — looking back — it was optimistic to believe that private financiers could have come up with the resources to surmount the challenge of the Alps. Moreover, the traffic offering was limited. In 1885 the West Coast had fewer than 30,000 people.

* * *

The line the Midland Railway Company did not finish building. Another shot of the preserved Ab 663, this time leaving Springfield on the Midland line and headed toward the Southern Alps of the South Island, the hills in the background showing the country to be tackled as the train heads toward the Otira tunnel through the mountains. (*Ron Sinclair*)

The New Zealand Midland Railway Company was floated in London with a capital of £500,000, the entire project cost being estimated at £2.5 million, with land grants being handed over by the government as the line progressed (land grants being a method widely use to encourage private railway construction in the United States). The company was to receive ten shillings of land for every pound spent on the project—which would have amounted to nearly 2.3 million hectares. Three months short of ten years after work began, the company had completed only 122 km of the line. The contract had required the completion of the entire project in that ten-year period.

In May 1893 the government took control of the project because of the company's failure to meet the terms of its contract; those holding debentures issued by the company fought (without success) the government's action as far as the Privy Council in London. This legal action further slowed work, and trains did not begin running to Otira until 1900.

Ocean Beach Railway Company

Length: 5.22 km.
Opened: 27 October 1876 to Andersons Bay; completely opened 25 December 1877.
Passenger services: Built primarily for passenger traffic in the form of race and excursion trains and opening up new areas to housing.
Status: Closed 1942.

The Dunedin, Peninsula and Ocean Beach Railway Company was established in 1874 with a capital of £60,000, with the intention of building two railway lines in the Dunedin area, one to the coast at the suburb of St Kilda and another to run along the harbour side of Otago Peninsula. Only the former was completed, although a short spur at Andersons Bay was also built. The line left the NZR track near the suburban station of

Kensington and followed what is now Andersons Bay Road, turning right at St Kilda to run parallel to the foreshore as far as the Forbury Park race track.

The company promoters saw the line as opening up housing development close to the ocean beaches of Dunedin, but with the main revenue to come from carrying passengers to race meetings and agricultural shows, along with picnic outings. On race days more than 3,000 people would use the company's trains to get to Forbury Park. In 1886, the company tried to sell the line to the government for £11,500, but the NZR district engineer decided it was unsafe and thereupon prohibited government rolling stock using the company's track. ft was reported that much of the operation was in disrepair, with decaying sleepers and station buildings.

Meanwhile, new horse-tram services to St Clair and Ocean Beach were taking away much of the railway's patronage. In 1888 the line passed into the control of the Dunedin City & Suburban Tramway Company, but race trains operated on the line for some years after that. In 1904 it came under the ownership of the Dunedin City Corporation.

The main use of the railway thereafter was to take livestock to the annual A&P Show at Tahuna — the last of these ran in 1938. But other trains did run: for example, in 1914 a special train carried troops from their camp at Tahuna to a waiting ship at Port Chalmers, and in 1922 a special ran from North Taieri (on the Outram branch) to Tahuna with horses for a sale.

The rail track survived until 1942, with part of the line in St Kilda sharing right of way with electric trams. This section was laid with three rails due to the differing railway (1,067 mm) and tramway (1,422 mm) gauges so that stock trains could move to and from Tahuna when shows were held. A short part of the track survived until 1949 and was used by NZR to store wagons.

The name of the Ocean Beach Railway lives on in the form of New Zealand's first operating railway museum along a line running parallel to St Kilda Beach, opened in 1961 by the Otago Railway & Locomotive Society.

Rakaia and Ashburton Forks Railway Company

The Rakaia and Ashburton Forks Railway Company was formed after the passage through parliament of the District Railways Act which allowed private companies to construct lines and levy rates on properties served by them. It was established with a capital of £100,000 in £50 shares, but only £65,640 of that was ever subscribed. The company planned initially to construct a line as far as Mt Somers but this idea was abandoned (a separate Mt Somers branch would be opened by NZR in 1889) and the location known as Ashburton Forks (later called Methven and now a substantial provincial centre) was chosen because six roads met there. However, landowners opposed to the plan set up a rival enterprise, the Rakaia, Mt Hutt and Alford Forest Railway Company by which they intended to build a separate line until that plan was thwarted by the local county council.

Meanwhile, the Rakaia & Ashburton Forks line saw the first sod turned on 19 November 1878. The branch, when completed in 1880, extended 35.56 km and had nine stations. Two

Rogers 2-4-4 Q class tank locomotives and three passenger cars were imported from the United States, while the goods wagons were built in New Zealand. The locomotives, later designated 'Q' class by NZR, were basically a tank version of the Rogers K class bought by NZR (of which one has been restored by the Plains Vintage Railway at Ashburton.

The 1881 timetable provided for mixed trains each way daily except Sunday. The down trains left Methven at 6.30 am and 4.50 pm with 1 hr 25 min being allowed for each trip. Up trains departed Rakaia at 9.00 am and 6.55 pm. The company was squeezed financially because the majority of local farmers refused to pay their rates; of the £10,000 in total levied by the company, only £600 had been collected by 1884. In 1881 the company reported a loss of £1,650 17s 2d. After a settlers' petition was sent to the government in Wellington, the Colonial Treasurer, Sir Julius Vogel, offered the company £75,000 for the line, which offer was accepted. After the sale was finalised on 1 April 1885 the government moved to cut costs by raising charges and eliminating some services. Race day trains were abolished, as was the daily mail service to Methven.

The branch, by now named Methven, lost its passenger services from 7 September 1958 and the line closed to all traffic on 31 July 1976.

Thames Valley and Rotorua Railway Company

The early European settlers of Rotorua were, like their counterparts elsewhere in the colony, eager for a rail connection. The initial agitation was for a light railway to Tauranga and in 1882 the Tauranga, East Coast and Hot Lakes Railway Company was formed to build a private line but it failed to raise the necessary capital in London. In 1886 a successor, the Tauranga (New Zealand) Railway Company was formed but this, too, eventually collapsed.

However, as government land purchases continued through the southern Waikato it had become obvious that the rail connection would be from that direction, not from Tauranga. This realisation threw up another hopeful private builder, the Thames Valley and Rotorua Railway Company; it secured backing with comparative ease, the lure being the opening up of the Rotorua lakes area to tourists travelling from Auckland. The company had been formed by a group of Auckland businessmen who had become frustrated by the government's unwillingness to build a railway link to Rotorua.

Work began on the line south Morrinsville in February 1882 and the section was opened as far as Tirau on 8 March 1886; the line reached Lichfield in June that year. The company was then taken over by the government and NZR operated the line thereafter. The 109.74 km line from Morrinsville was completed on 8 December 1894.

Waimate Railway Company

When the government completed the short (7.42 km) branch from Studholme Junction to Waimate, South Canterbury, in 1877 rresidents further inland formed the Waimate Railway Company to extend the line. This they did, opening 11.27 km of what was known as the Waimate Gorge Railway by February 1883 as far as Waihao Forks, and then a further 2.05 km to Waihao Downs ten weeks later, with trains operated by NZR. In 1885 the government agreed to buy the company and thereafter operated the entire line. The company had completed another long section of formation but lines were never laid on that.

The official opening of the first section of the company's line was celebrated in the good shed at Waihao Downs. The company had spent £29,062 to reach that point. An Otago Daily Times reporter described his train trip through the gorge:

> As the train winds its way between the high hills on either side the suggestion forces itself upon the traveller that he is to be plunged into a mountainous country, remarkable rather for its wild scenery than anything else. Outcroppings of stone are seen on every hand and the scant vegetation is relieved only by tall, gaunt-looking cabbage trees and the stream which hurries alongside the line … After two and a half miles of rather slow travelling, the train emerges on to land of the character of that left behind on entering the gorge and the sudden change is somewhat bewildering. To the north lies country which at once suggests good growing properties and on the other side undulating hills afford fine pasture for sheep.

On the day of the opening, some 300 people left Waimate on the special train and the 'excellent' lunch included patriotic toasts.

The company had been formed with a capital of £100,000 but the contractor proposed to build the formation, including a bridge, for £10,615. The cost of the survey, including rails, stations and sleepers, brought the total up to the £29,062 figure. The company was very pleased it completed it works for £3,522 13s 4d per mile, compared to what it claimed was the average £6,500 per mile spent by the government laying railways around New Zealand.

Passenger services with withdrawn from the Waimate branch in 1931. The line built by the company beyond Waimate closed on 11 December 1953 and the remainder of the branch — that built by NZR — on 1 April 1966.

Waimea Plains Railway Company

Length: 59.07 km.
Opened: 31 July 1880.
Passenger services: Withdrawn 17 September 1945, although Christmas and Easter holiday specials operated until 1959.
Status: Purchased by NZR 13 November 1886; Gore-Balfour closed 1 April 1971; Balfour-Lumsden closed 15 January 1978.

This rail line between Gore and Lumsden was constructed by the Waimea Plains Railway Company, whose directors were all well known southern business figures (including the Dunedin politician William Larnach). Its head office was in Dunedin. Invercargill business leaders saw the line as a ploy by Dunedin interests to tap the trade of western Southland. The prospectus issued sought to raise £150,000 and promised that the line would become 'one of the best paying lines in the Colony', by bringing Kingston (at the southern tip of Lake Wakitipu) within eight and a half hours of Dunedin and would also open up new agricultural areas. However, at the dissolution of the company it was found that there were seventy-five shareholders who had subscribed a total of just £35,610, the rest of the development capital having been raised by way of loans. The cost of construction, using local contractors, was £108,713.

The line was opened in 1880, with the company purchasing two locomotives, F36 and F37. The company owned no other rolling stock, paying NZR at the rate of a penny per mile for the hire of wagons running over the line. The government provided a £9 subsidy for each passenger service operated between Lumsden and Gore, with fares charged on the same scale as NZR's. Passenger services were designed to connect with NZR services at both Lumsden and Gore, although this arrangement ended on 31 December 1883, after the company failed to continue providing the connecting services required by NZR. There was the additional inconvenience for through passengers in having to purchase new tickets when they arrived at either Gore or Lumsden, there being no through ticketing system. Another peculiarity of line was the absence of nameboards at the stations, so that local knowledge was essential to know when you had reached your destination. An account left by one excursionist in 1882 reports that departure was made from Dunedin at 6.15 am, with the traveller reaching Kingston at 3.00 pm and the steamer *Mountaineer* meeting the train to take passengers across the lake to Queenstown.

The operation of the line was profitable initially, with the company declaring a surplus of £964 for the first year, although subsequently the directors were forced to apply to the government for permission to levy rates on landowners under the District Railways Act of 1878. But, not unexpectedly, the landowners refused to pay these rates; by the time the government purchased the line on 13 November 1886, expensive legal proceedings had managed to extract only half the rated amount due to the company.

The government took over operating the line a year before it assumed ownership. The Royal Commission on Railways had recommended against the government buying the Waimea Plains railway on the grounds that, had it been built as a government line, it would followed a quite different route; as it was, the line passed through areas largely devoid of population of any size. This shortage of local customers was illustrated at the 1884 annual meeting where shareholders were told that operations that year had resulted in a loss of more than £600.

The government bought the Waimea Plains railway as a going concern for £100,000. In October 1887 the original company was wound up at a loss to shareholders of £1 18s 0d a share. When NZR took over, farmers complained that some stations did not have goods sheds and they were suffering losses due to flour, sugar and other supplies being left on uncovered station platforms and being ruined by rain. A goods shed was provided at Mandeville.

In its latter years, losses kept on mounting. In its last year, the deficit was $17,000. Most of the line was closed as of 1 April 1971, the Balfour-Lumsden section remaining open for another seven years to service wheat traffic, but that business did not live up to expectations.

Wellington and Manawatu Railway Company

Length: 135 km
Opened: 3 November 1886
Status: Acquired by New Zealand Railways on 7 December 1908

While railways had been built through the Wairarapa to Hawke's Bay and northwards from Palmerston North to Wanganui, the government in Wellington did not consider a direct route from the capital to the Manawatu to be a high priority. Indeed, it was believed that the intended connection via the Manawatu Gorge and Wairarapa would be quite satisfactory, seeing that much of the countryside on the coast route was viewed as having low agricultural potential; the WMR directors, however, saw the potential of the area once the swamps were drained. The economic depression of the 1880s led to a further deferral of consideration of the coastal route. A royal commission had also advised the government that the building of a Manawatu line was not justifiable.

A Wellington and Manawatu Railway Company train leaving the old Thorndon station at Wellington in 1897. The harbour area to the left of the train was eventually reclaimed and would accommodate the large railway yards and the Aotea Quay wharf to service overseas shipping. (*Bob Stott collection*)

Thus, a group of Wellington businessmen was brought together in 1881 to form a joint stock company with the intent of building a privately owned railway. The government came to their aid by passing the Railways Construction and Land Act to make it legally possible for such a line to be built, and the Wellington & Manawatu Railway Company was registered with capital of £500,000, that later being increased to £850,000. The government then offered a land grant of about 85,000 hectares, valued at £96,000, and even handed over an iron bridge; the company subsequently used it to cross the neck of Porirua Harbour.

The WMR laid 135 km of track between Wellington and Longburn, the latter on the southern outskirts of what would become the city of Palmerston North. The route still exists today except for the first 13.75 km of present-day track out of the capital. That section out of Wellington, with its very tight curves, was bypassed in 1937 by the NZR for a straighter section which involved drilling two tunnels; the old line was then truncated at the suburb of Johnsonville and has since served as a branch line for commuter trains to that part of Wellington.

Apart from negotiating the swampy areas further to the north, WMR needed to build thirteen tunnels between Wellington and Paekakariki, a distance of 39 km, in addition to the Belmont viaduct, a 37-metre-high structure (the viaduct was also made redundant by the 1937 deviation). Five other bridges were required.

The last spike was driven by Governor Sir William Jervois on 3 November 1886 at Otaihanga (between Waikanae and Paraparaumu). From 1902 an agreement was reached between the company and NZR allowing through workings between Wellington and New Plymouth, removing the need for passengers to change trains at Longburn.

Among WMR's many achievements was the introduction of New Zealand's first dining car in 1886. However, the lack of end platforms to connect with adjacent carriages meant passengers could access or leave it only at stations rather than en route. In 1890 a conventional dining car with end platforms was built from an existing carriage, thus overcoming the access problem. WMR was twelve years ahead of NZR in this move, but it was thirty years ahead of the state railway when it introduced electric lighting in carriages in 1896, using storage batteries. The company also used telephones along the line, rather than NZR's Morse code system.

The railway had a distinctly American look to it, from the style of the locomotives to the US-built bogie wagons and clerestory-roofed carriages. The locomotives were of American design and manufacture and, along with green and red painted cars, the appearance of WMR trains was in striking contrast to NZR's consists. In all, the company owned fifty-three carriages, many built in the United States. Even second-class cars were well appointed with padded seats, compared with NZR where many carriages still had wooden ones.

In 1927 New Zealand Railway Magazine pointed out that the Wellington and Manawatu Railway Company employed wood instead of coal on their tender engines running between Paekakariki and Longburn, 'not only because of the economies resulting by its use, but as being an important factor in the disposal of the bush lands owned by the company. The annual saving in firing with the wood burning machines was estimated at between £300 and £400 per loco. Later, two larger "consolidation" 2–8–0 type locos were converted to burn wood fuel and the amount of wood required was more than double what was previously necessary. The supply was the means of assisting very materially the settlers or those who purchased the company's lands, as perhaps the greater part of the land was then virgin bush'. The use of firewood was discontinued in the summer months in order to avoid the risk of sparks causing fires in the bush.

WMR operated profitably for much of its short existence but within three years of start-up had closed several smaller flag stations that produced inadequate revenue. All trains were mixed, including the New Plymouth Mail worked in conjunction with NZR. The 1905 working timetable showed that WMR ran seven trains a day Monday to Friday out of Wellington, with additional services some days just as far as Johnsonville. The day at its Thorndon station began with the 6.30 am to Johnsonville, then the 7.50 am, 10.10 am, 1.20 pm and 4.15 pm trains to Longburn, followed by the 5.20 pm to Johnsonville and 6.20 pm to Paekakariki. In addition, there was a 6.40 am Paekakariki-Longburn service.

* * *

7

INSTRUCTIONS FOR TRAIN WORK AND SHUNTING AT INTERMEDIATE STATIONS.

No. 1 train will shunt where required.

No. 2 train will shunt where required, and will take to Longburn any loaded wagons at Makerua and Linton that are South bound.

No. 3 train will shunt Tokomaru, Shannon, Kereru, Manakau, and Waikanae.

No. 4 train will not shunt except by special instructions. Load should not exceed 30 from Paekakariki.

No. 5 train will put off loaded wagons at Linton, and will shunt at Levin, Ohau, Otaki, and Paraparaumu, and pick up any loaded South bound wagons at Te Horo.

No. 6 train will shunt where required North of Paekakariki (except Manakau, Shannon, Makerua, Tokomaru, and Linton), and will shunt out all loaded South bound wagons at Te Horo.

No. 7 train will not shunt except to put off live stock at Johnsonville. Load not to exceed 30 from Longburn.

No. 8 train will pick up empty stock wagons at Johnsonville and shunt at Porirua only.

No. 9 train will shunt at Shannon, Levin, Otaki, and Waikanae.

No. 10 train will shunt at Shannon only.

Nos. 11, 12, 13, 15, 16, 19, and 20 trains will shunt as required.

No. 14 train will not shunt at Crofton, Khandallah, or Porirua, but will shunt elsewhere as required.

On Saturdays only empty train will be coupled to No. 10 from Wellington to Plimmerton, returning from there as No. 13 train.

It must be understood that none of the foregoing instructions prohibit trains (except Nos. 4 and 7) from working other stations and sidings than those specified, provided engine power and time permits. Trains should not run lightly loaded, if loads can be got without causing trains to run late.

Reporting Loads on Trains.

Guards of all South bound trains must hand to Stationmaster, Otaki, daily, a schedule giving description, contents, and destination of all vehicles on their trains.

Care must be taken to state particularly any trucks containing perishable goods.

Stationmaster, Otaki, will telephone these schedules to Paekakariki immediately after trains leave his station.

Similar schedules of all North bound trains will be telephoned from Wellington to Station-master, Paekakariki, immediately after departure of each train.

Just a few of the many and precise instructions for staff contained in the Wellington and Manawatu Railway Company's working timetable.

★ ★ ★

6
Railways at Work

Industrial Lines and Sidings

FIFTY OR MORE YEARS AGO train travellers in New Zealand would have seen a succession of rail tracks curving off into timber mills, freezing works, fertiliser plants and oil depots. Alternatively, they passed sidings that clearly served a line-side factory; at Petone the Austin car plant had a siding and loading bank at the southern end of the yard, while General Motors used a siding at its plant between Petone and Ava stations. The Ford Motors siding ran off the Gracefield branch.

Many industrial sidings could be seen along the line between Greymouth and Otira, including those owned by the Greymouth Power Board, State Coal Mines and the Te Kingi Land and Timber Company. Indeed, at virtually every station on that section there was a bush tramway branching off. A traveller on the Christchurch-Invercargill expresses would have noted the Temuka Milling Company's private siding at that station, the Canterbury Frozen Meat Co's siding at Pareora, or the Southland Tanneries' private siding just out of Mataura.

The great majority of these industrial sidings or lines have now disappeared, either because the industry has closed or the switch to road transport has been made. But, in their heyday, these sidings accounted for much of the bustle on New Zealand's railway system before the era of bulk tonnage and non-stop main line running.

Meat freezing companies were among the heavy users of rail, both for the transport inwards of the doomed livestock and for the shipment outwards of the frozen carcasses. In Wellington, for example, both the Wellington Meat Export Company at Ngauranga (with its miniscule Barclay 0-4-0 locomotive) and the Gear Meat Company at Petone had extensive rail operations. Most of the smaller operations, including the Patea Freezing Company, also had their own private sidings. The Auckland Farmers Freezing Company has had numerous rail operations complete with its own shunting locomotives, including those at Moerewa, near Otiria in Northland, at two wharves in Auckland, at the Southdown freezing works in Auckland, at Horotiu north of Hamilton, at Rangiuru near Te Puke and later at works bought in 1989 at Wanganui, Fielding, Wairoa and on the outskirts of Masterton.

Dairy factories have been another source of private sidings, such as the Waikato Dairy Co-operative at Hautapu on the Cambridge branch, or the Rangitaiki Plains Dairy Company private siding at Edgecumbe in the Bay of Plenty.

The proliferation of small timber mills around the country saw timber loaded at hundreds of points along the NZR system. Most of these sidings produced modest quantity to be carried by NZR trains but some operations were on a much more impressive scale, such as that which was operated by Tasman Pulp and Paper's plant at Kawerau where the company operated its own large shunting locomotives until 1998.

The most spectacular example was the Whakatane Board Mills, which laid a private line from the East Coast Main Trunk into its Whakatane plant. This industrial line was opened in 1939. It was built to link the Matahina Tramway via a short section of NZR line to the company's own 11 km line between the East Coast Main Trunk with the company's Whakatane-based plant. Log trains operated on the line in conjunction with the Matahina Tramway (1930-1966), a line that provided access to the vast timber resources inland from the Bay of Plenty. Typically, the WBM log trains would travel the company's own line from Whakatane, traverse the NZR line as far as Edgecumbe, then turn into the tramway (the train having to carry an NZR guard when on government tracks). From 1949 the tramway section was worked only by diesel locomotives, the New Zealand Forest Service that year banning steam engines in its forests. WBM had bought two Drewry 0-6-0 locomotives (similar to NZR's Ds shunters).

In the 1950s and 1960s there was considerable lobbying from Whakatane interests to have the government take over the WBM line and provide services into the town, and when an enthusiast special using an 88-seater Fiat railcar arrived down the company line in 1961 it was met by the mayor and local business leaders. Services on the line were later controlled from Kawerau, with trains passing the Awakeri shopping centre reduced to 5 km/h.

Ports and mines required the building of industrial sidings. At Wellington, lines ran on to several of the main wharves, with tracks crossing the Waterloo Quay road from the main yards to run on to Aotea Quay, Pipitea, Kings and Glasgow wharfs. Container traffic required that all the main ports maintain rail networks into their areas. A few kept their own motive power, as did Timaru Harbour Board with its Wd locomotive. Until 1957 Napier Harbour Board operated two locomotives from the NZR terminus on the Ahuriri branch to wharf-side. The Port Whangarei Port branch ran 2.25km from Whangarei yards to the wharf sidings at the port.

Coal mining companies were important operators of both locomotive and industrial lines. State Coal Mines operated the Glen Massey line in the Waikato. On the Glen Afton branch (later the Rotowaro industrial line) the department ran twice-daily passenger services for miners as well as hauling coal, and also ran an all-carriage train on the Pukemiro spur. In the South Island the Mines Department operated the Roa-Blackball section beyond NZR's terminus on the Blackball branch. Further south the Kaitangata Railway & Coal Company and the Ohai Railway Board were both operating fleets of locomotives over their private lines with NZR motive power taking over for the state-owned sections of branches.

The Kaitangata operation was established in 1872 as Kaitangata Coal Company, then reconstructed as the Kaitangata

Railway and Coal Company in 1875. Its 5.95 km line, when it passed to the Mines Department in 1956, had the distinction of being the oldest privately owned railway in New Zealand. Its construction was made possible when the South Island main trunk reached the banks of the Clutha River on 16 June 1876. The following day the company's own branch came into operation, its trains running to the NZR station at Stirling. There was also a short spur line to the Castle Hill mine. The line did have some competition until 1883: until that year small vessels continued to come up the Clutha and load coal. The company's own mine closed in 1959, but the Mines Department had taken control of the railway three years previously and continued to operate trains until the line was closed on 30 December 1970. An F class locomotive, manufactured by Sharp, Stewart and Company for the Kaitangata line, is now preserved at Shantytown Museum on the West Coast.

Industrial sidings ranged in scope and importance from New Zealand Steel's at Mission Bush to that owned by a pottery at Benhar, north of Balclutha. At the latter, trains shunted clay wagons into the siding and pulled out with box wagons loaded with toilet pans (the pottery being the sole manufacturer of these in New Zealand). This siding was closed after the pottery was destroyed by fire in 1990.

Electrification

Otira–Arthur's Pass: 13.97km, 4 August 1923–1 November 1997 (date of last official working)

Christchurch-Lyttelton: 9.77 km, 14 February 1929 until 18 September 1970

Johnsonville branch: 10.49 km, 2 July 1938

Wellington-Paekakariki: 38.8 km, June 1940, extended to Paraparaumu in 1983, then total 48.3 km when extended to Waikanae 2011.

Wellington-Taita: 20.55 km, 14 September 1953, 32.4 km when extended to Upper Hutt 1955

Gracefield branch: 2.57km, 14 September 1953 until 1983

Hutt Valley Junction-Melling: 1.37 km, 23 November 1953; to Melling, 3 km, 1 March 1954

Te Rapa-Palmerston North: 411 km, 24 June 1988.

Auckland suburban system: in process of being electrified.

The first line to lose its electric overhead wires was the Lyttelton-Christchurch section.

Until the central section of the North Island Main Trunk between Te Rapa and Palmerston North was electrified in 1988, electric traction in New Zealand had been confined to less than 120 km — and that in five separate sections of track. These were the suburban rail lines in Wellington (to Johnsonville, Upper Hutt, the Gracefield branch, Melling brach and Paraparaumu on the North Island Main Trunk), Lyttelton-Christchurch and Otira-Arthur's Pass. Both the latter sections have now been converted to diesel-only haulage and the overhead lines removed. Electrification was also removed from the Gracefield branch in Wellington but was extended on the NIMT from Paraparaumu to Waikanae.

The first electrified railway in New Zealand was the 13.97 km stretch of line running from Arthur's Pass to Otira through the Otira tunnel, opened in 1923.

Electric locomotive backs on to its suburban train at Lyttelton station in November 1970. (*Bob Stott*)

In February 1946 the Minister of Railways, Bob Semple, announced that all suburban rail services between Wellington and the Hutt Valley were to be electrified, with Upper Hutt to be served by a duplicated line via Waterloo and Taita. The multiple-unit electric sets (soon known simply as "units" by Wellingtonians) went into service to Johnsonville in 1938 and then were introduced after the end of the Second World War to other lines in the Wellington area to the Wellington-Paekakariki run.

Several investigations have been undertaken over the years into various electrification proposals (and still they come: there has been agitation to extend the Wellington suburban wiring to Otaki on the North Island Main Trunk and Featherstone on the Wairarapa line as people commute into Wellington from farther afield). In 1925 the government commissioned the British consultants Merz and McLellan who recommended that electrification be undertaken on Auckland, Wellington and Christchurch suburban tracks (with the possibility of including the Dunedin area). Among the report's conclusions was that if the existing Main Trunk via Johnsonville were electrified, it would make unnecessary the Tawa Flat deviation for the then foreseeable future. The report also recommended that the old line to Upper Hutt via Haywards be electrified, as well as the then branch to Naenae on the other side of the Hutt River; in Auckland that the electric overhead be built out to Henderson and Otahuhu; in Christchurch northward to Rangiora and through the Lyttelton tunnel. The Dunedin option would have seen electrification from Port Chalmers to Mosgiel. If that were done, the report said, it might be worth extending the electric system to the difficult climb out of Sawyers Bay and through the Mihiwaka tunnel on the main line northwards from Dunedin.

In 1950 the then general manager of NZR, F. W. Aickin, produced a report entitled Electrification of the North Island Main Trunk Railway. It recommended the immediate commitment to electrifying the Paekakariki-Auckland line, with wires to be strung over 655 route kilometres and 996 track kilometres. The study had been triggered by the postwar coal crisis, when NZR was reliant for its steam locomotives on both imported oil and coal, as local production of the latter was inadequate for its requirements. Aickin proposed to contract British Insulated Callenders Cables to install the electrification, with locomotives to be supplied by the English Electric Co. While the existing Wellington-Paekakariki section was electrified at 1500v dc, Aickin recommended that the NIMT use between 16,000 and 20,000v ac (with the short section from Paekakariki to the capital to be converted after its rolling stock was due for replacement). Aickin estimated that the conversion of the NIMT would pay for itself in nine years, both in terms of fuel savings and the removal of the constrictions on the NIMT capacity (resulting from limits on the loads due to steam operation). The report also suggested consideration of light electric railcars for passenger services on the NIMT. However, the government decided instead to opt for diesel, with orders being placed in November 1950 for the DF and DC diesel-electric machines.

But the most ambitious electrification project in New Zealand railway history was that for the central section of the North Island Main Trunk between Palmerston North and Te Rapa.

The oil shock of the early 1970s was one of the factors that provoked consideration of the plan. After calling in the Japanese Railway Technical Service for advice, the government decided in 1981 to proceed, with the cost being estimated at $260 million.

Tender documents for the electrification of 411 km of the NIMT were released in March 1983, with the first stage to be Palmerston North-Ohakune. Meanwhile, NZR ordered twenty-two electric locomotives from Brush Electrical Machines of the United Kingdom; each possessed the capacity to haul 1,000-tonne trains up the steepest grades on the trunk. The opportunity was taken to improve some of the central sections of the line, including a new 8.5 km deviation between Ohakune and Horopito, a section that included the new Hapuawhenua viaduct built in reinforced concrete. Other bridges were rebuilt to take the heavier loads, while tunnels were either 'daylighted' or had their floors lowered (as in the case of the tunnels on the Raurimu spiral) to accommodate the new locomotives and the overhead catenary. More than 10,000 concrete poles had to be erected to hold the overhead wires.

In March 1987 electric power was first switched on between Palmerston North and Bunnythorpe with commercial operation beginning as far as Tauramarunui, then extending to Te Rapa in 1988.

Guards

These passengers look a little too well dressed for second-class ticket holders in this posed **NZR** photo taken in the 1950s. But the guard is real — once a familiar figure on all New Zealand trains, passenger and goods; but as passenger services were cut back, and goods trains operated without guard's vans, their number become very few, confined to suburban and the few reaming long-distance passenger trains. Most guards had a cheery word for passengers as they moved along clipping tickets. As there were no intercom systems on long distance trains in the steam era, they also walked the length of their trains announcing each refreshment stop ahead. (*NZR—Bob Stott collection*)

Once a familiar sight on New Zealand's railways, guards are seen now only on passenger trains, although now they are called train conductors. For most of the railway era in New Zealand and until the 1980s no train (other than shunts) ran without a guard on board. The job originally was one of being brake men with the van in which they rode always placed at the rear of the train so the guard could apply the brakes to help slow or stop the train. The introduction of automatic braking systems eliminated this part of the guard's duties and, thereafter, the guard's van was not required to be at the rear of the train (but usually was).

NZR and the Wellington and Manawatu Railway Company laid down strict requirements for guards. For example, in the WMR's 1891 set of regulations required that guards be able to read and write, that they carry always a reliable watch and a copy of the working timetable, and be responsible for ensuring that trains were in full working order (including checks on couplings, lamps and that tarpaulins were firmly tied down) before train departure. Once under way, the train was under the control of the guard. The driver and fireman were to follow any instructions given by the guard.

The 1905 WMR working timetable included multiple instructions for guards. At intermediate stations they were required to check any wagons being added to the train to ensure no water could damage the contents and they were expected to supervise loading and unloading of goods in less than wagon loads. The guards were instructed to call out the names of the stations as the train stopped at platforms. Another demand was that the brake van be kept clean at all times. They had to make sure points and stop-blocks were locked when departing flag stations (where no staff were based) and that wagons not be left on sidings at those flag stations longer than was necessary. And they certainly were to make sure that their writing on consignment notes was fully legible.

In egalitarian New Zealand, the differences between ranks were often blurred. Here the guard and the fireman refuel We 375 at Rewanui while the driver watches, hands on hips. The locomotive had been converted from a B class tender engine to a tank engine (4-6-4T) in 1943, and became one of only three We class locomotives. The Rewanui branch served a coal mine inaccessible by road, so apart from the coal trains, these locomotives hauled carriages taking the miners to and from work. (*NZR—Bob Stott collection*)

Level Crossings

Rail lines throughout New Zealand were built, from the earliest days of government involvement, on the basis that money being spent on 'extras' should be avoided where possible. It was necessary to build bridges to span rivers, but not to cross roads. Thus New Zealand's rail network went for level crossings (the road traffic gave way) or the road-rail bridge (again, the road traffic gave way). Both were a familiar feature — and a frequent source of danger. In January 2001 this was again shown when the Southerner ploughed into a truck on a level crossing at Makakihi south of Timaru.

Over the years bridges have been built on main roads where they intersect with railways, which has done much to relieve the pressure on train drivers. In the early 1950s, for example, one of the first flyovers was built (at Petone), replacing a level crossing at one of the busiest sections of lines in New Zealand; dozens of passenger trains each day plus multiple freight workings had until then frequent frequent lowering of the barriers on a busy road. Many country level crossings have disappeared, thanks mainly to branch line closures, but it is extraordinary how many level crossings remain along main lines.

In earlier times, many busy road level crossings were manned by a crossing keeper who, on the approach of a train, would stand in the road with a 'Stop' sign. The express trains pulling out of Christchurch would traverse many level crossings in the inner city area, each with its own crossing keeper; at crossings such as Durham Street, Montreal Street, Antigua Road, Grove

Road and Lincoln Road, the keepers would emerge from their huts as the trains approached. The last of these huts, near Sockburn station, was made redundant in 1959 by the construction of a road over bridge.

The first railways, indeed, were equipped with gates at level crossings that physically barred road traffic. But many of these also required a gatekeeper's cottage, another expense which Vogel thought unnecessary given his cost-saving plan to built railways that could be used only at low speeds.

Now, crossings have either bells or simple signs; only the more important have arms which descend on a train's approach. Without the arms providing a physical barrier, however, safety is in the hands of road users, and this has proved to be an unreliable system with drivers either not bothering to slow down at crossings, or even impatiently racing to get ahead of an approaching train. And, with the withdrawal of four-wheeled wagons, all trains in New Zealand now travel on average at speeds far higher than fifty years ago, a factor which further heightens the dangers involved.

Ports and Wharves

Ports were the initial linchpins of the New Zealand railway system. Most of the earliest lines were built to bring an effective transport link between the nearest port and its immediate hinterland: hence, some of the first priorities for railways included lines from the nearest large town to the wharves — to Onehunga in the case of Auckland, to Wellington from the Hutt Valley,

Kawakawa in Northland to a wharf at Tuamarere, from New Plymouth to Taranaki's then premier port at Waitara, Napier to its port. In the south, Westland's first lines were built to transport coal to the wharf-side in Greymouth and Westport, while Bluff, Port Chalmers and Lyttelton were all among the earliest rail connections in the South Island.

Being an export-oriented economy, New Zealand's ports have continued to rely heavily on rail. Even as late as the mid-1990s, about seventy per cent of all export cargoes shipped through Wellington arrived at the port by rail.

A more recent development was the concept of inland ports. The Port of Tauranga in 1999 established a dry port near Onehunga, Auckland. Named Metroport, and based at the Southdown Freight Terminal, it relied on the rail system to carry cargo to and from the wharves at Mt Maunganui. The capacity of the operation was shown in its early days when nine trains ran to Auckland over one weekend, carrying containers which had been unloaded at Tauranga. Port of Tauranga developed the concept to tap business from the highly industrialised areas of South Auckland.

In its time, NZR controlled a number of wharves, including the main passenger jetty at Onehunga, the wharves at Foxton and Queenstown wharf, the latter the only official railway station in New Zealand not connected to the railway network (NZR operating the steamers on Lake Wakitipu). The building of the Foxton branch line (31.2 km-long) was justified by the need for transport to and from the port there to service the city of Palmerston North at a time when the roads between the two were poor due to the swampy terrain in much of the area. Moreover heavy loads of coal had to moved to Palmerston North from colliers berthed at Foxton after a run up the coast from Westport. Apart from that, the port was also a busy one while the flax industry flourished.

Road Limits

The viability of the comparatively dense railway system, with its main lines and many branches, was artificially sustained from 1936 when the first Labour government introduced a thirty-mile road limit. The effect of this was that no goods could be carried by lorry for more than thirty miles if there was a railway line available. In 1961 the National government extended the limit to forty miles, and then in 1977 it was further extended to 150 km (or 93.3 miles). In 1983 the road industry was deregulated and the road limit protecting NZR traffic disappeared.

Sleepers

Timber sleepers were typically laid 2,400 to the mile on the NZR system, equivalent to 1,493 per kilometre. As railways penetrated into areas with dense bush, timber was cut for sleepers; for example, several small townships grew as the rails pressed northward to Napier through southern Hawke's Bay, with local totara stands providing the timber for sleepers. Between 1879 and 1899, eighteen million sleepers were despatched from just one small station on the line (Makotuku). In the Waikato the puriri forests around Waiuku provided the timber for large quantities of sleepers used on rail construction around Auckland. (Puriru is a hardwood that, even without treatment, will endure for about fifty years in the ground.)

For much of the twentieth century sleepers for the New Zealand network were cut from more durable Australian hardwoods. In addition NZR, in the 1960s, began using treated and locally-grown radiata pine. Concrete sleepers were introduced in the 1970s.

Workshops

Over its existence NZR operated thirteen main workshops. The high number was the result of the early fragmented nature of the New Zealand railway system and it's the many isolated sections — hence workshops were needed in Greymouth in the days before the Otira tunnel connected the West Coast with Canterbury (and thus the rest of the NZR system). In the North Island there were once workshops at Auckland (Newmarket and Otahuhu), East Town (at Wanganui), Sentry Hill near New Plymouth, Napier and Wellington (first Petone, then Hutt). The South Island, apart from Hillside in Dunedin which survived until 2012, once had workshops at Addington in Christchurch, Elmer Lane in Greymouth, Westport and Invercargill.

The Canterbury Provincial Government opened a railway workshop in Christchurch in 1863 to service its equipment until the lines and rolling stock passed to the central government in 1876 upon abolition of the provincial authorities. Hillside came into existence in 1875, followed by Petone, Addington and East Town.

The once famous Hillside railway workshops in Dunedin have now been closed but one of their last major projects was the construction in 2011 of new Scenic AK class carriages for KiwiRail's long-distance trains. Here the cars are seen negotiating the Raurima Spiral in the mountainous central North Island. (*Roy Sinclair*)

There had been mounting concern in the late 1890s and the early years of the twentieth century about the inadequacies of the workshops, including their obsolete equipment. NZR was forced, due to the lack of capacity at the workshops back then, to import eighty-nine locomotives, sixty-three carriages and about 1,000 wagons from overseas. A turning point came in 1924 with the Fay-Raven Commission on Railways, which recommended the existing plants should be improved or replaced and that £2.75 million be spent on this. The commission concluded the existing workshops were using out-of-date machinery, and the operation of the plants was unsatisfactory in many respects. In the case of Newmarket, the commission commented on the poor line layout causing a bottleneck. As a consequence, East Town, Addington and Hillside were expanded, and new workshops were built at Otahuhu and Hutt. Petone and Newmarket were closed. Locomotive building was concentrated on Hutt and Hillside, the former also looking after electrical work and signalling. The end result was that the network of workshops was modernised and, apart from the contracts let to A&G Price (the private engineering company based in Thames) NZR had become self-sufficient in most areas of railway equipment by the 1930s.

Indeed, the strengthening of the system following the 1924 report was such that the workshops were capable of playing a significant part in New Zealand's war effort between 1939 and 1945. They turned out Bren gun carriers, bomb casings, marine engines and naval boilers among other essential items.

Newmarket workshops in Auckland were in full operation by 1885, the new plant being necessary to cope with all the locomotives and rolling stock on the then isolated Auckland section. But the workshops were located on a site that did not easily allow for expansion, and the Fay-Raven report highlighted the need to find a better location. By 1928 the new Hutt and Otahuhu workshops had been approved. By this time, of course, Auckland had been connected to the North Island network so it was possible for NZR to allocate car and wagon work to Otahuhu (although some minor steam locomotive repairs were carried out there initially) and locomotive work to Hutt. When Otahuhu opened in late 1928, it was equipped with shops for blacksmiths, machine work and wagon building, along with two car shops. Over the years, Otahuhu built a wide range of rolling stock including the Aa suburban carriages, the observation cars for the Rotorua Limited and express carriages, including sleeping cars, as well as outfitting the Royal train in 1953. Major locomotive work was undertaken at Otahuhu from 1947 when it was used for converting K and Ka class engines to oil burning. With dieselisation, Otahuhu was called on for locomotive and railcar repairs. Otahuhu workshops were closed on 30 June 1992 as part of workshop rationalisation.

Addington was commissioned in 1880, and the workshops inherited from the Canterbury Provincial Government near the then Christchurch station were transferred to the new site. By 1889 Addington was building locomotives with an order for two 2-6-2 W class engines. In 1894 these workshops produced the first tender locomotive built by NZR to its own design, the U class. Then came many of the best-known types of NZR locomotives: the A class was followed by the X engines in 1906. By 1915 Addington was building what would be for many years a mainstay of the NZR system, the Ab locomotives (one of which survives on the Kingston Flyer services, along with one built at Hillside). By 1926 the government decided that Addington would specialise in passenger carriages and goods wagons.

The East Town workshops in Wanganui were commissioned in 1880, a further extension of railway capacity following on from the Vogel public works programme. Two years previously, the line between Foxton and Wanganui had opened, and now the government turned its attention to completing the link to New Plymouth. The complex was built complete with locomotive erecting shop, machine shop, wood mill, blacksmith shop and attached boiler shop. Most of the work until 1900 involved the repair of rolling stock used in Taranaki and Hawke's Bay. After the 1924 Fay-Raven Commission, it was decided that East Town would concentrate on manufacturing points and crossings, along with tarpaulins. However, the points and crossings work was moved to Woburn in the early 1930s, the East Town staff reverting to repairing locomotives, carriages and brake vans. Over the following years East Town saw a wide variety of tasks, including manufacturing tools and velocipedes, building railway huts and making furniture for railway stations and offices. After World War II, the workshops did overhauls on shunting locomotives from across the North Island.

East Town workshops had the distinction of being the principle producer of tarpaulins for use on goods wagons, which were sent to stations all over the country from Okaihau to Bluff. The first 'tarps' were made of canvas, with the sheets and the lashing ropes coated in a mixture of linseed oil and vegetable black to condition them against the weather. Many of the early workers in this department were sailmakers by trade, and all the work was done by hand until 1915 when sewing machines were introduced. By 1928, with a new dedicated building and the transfer of additional staff from Newmarket workshops, East Town was producing at the rate of fifty tarpaulins a week. However, this factory was destroyed by fire in 1954, and tarpaulin makers at Addington workshops were forced to work double shifts to meet the demand throughout the NZR system until a replacement building was available at East Town. In 1973 NZR switched to PVC tarpaulins, which lasted longer and were cheaper to make, and running repairs could be made at any railway station with temporary patches. In the 1980 financial year, Wanganui produced 5,711 new PVC tarpaulins and repaired about 15,000 others. East Town closed in 1986 as NZR sought to rationalise its workshops. The government announced that a new workshop complex was to be built at a cost of $866,000 at Aramoho, Wanganui, but this is now also closed.

In 1986 Hutt workshops became the central motive power operation, the other workshops handling rolling stock. The Greymouth workshops closed that year, with the workload transferred to the Westport rolling stock depot. The need for two workshops on the Coast reflected the large numbers of locomotives and wagons required for coal haulage.

But, even in their last years, many of the workshops undertook a variety of tasks. As late as 1978 and 1979 the Greymouth and Westport workshops were still turning out new four-wheeled wagons (class MCC) designed to carry motor vehicles. But perhaps the gravest blow was the decision to close Hillside in Dunedin, made after it was decided to order new wagons from China, rolling stock that were plagued with technical problems. Hillside had a proud history: between 1897 and 1967 the plant built 190 locomotives, the best known of that output being the Ja steam locomotive.

7

Ghost Lines, Vanished Places

SOME BRANCH LINES EARNED a reprieve from early closure. One such was the Waikaka branch in Southland province, a 20.82 km railway that never really served any great purpose. It was opened in 1908, built only after the government extracted an undertaking that the farmers (who had complained about onerous carting of produce to the nearest main line station, McNab) agreed to purchase £50,000 in government debentures to offset the cost of the line — a seemingly prudent measure considering no actual towns lay along the route. But nothing deterred the people of Southland; in 1909 the Minister for Public Works, Roderick McKenzie, was on a tour of the area and was beseeched by a deputation asking that the branch be extended into even more sparsely settled country. McKenzie responded that there 'is a railway up every gully in Southland'. In 1912 the coal pit at Waikaka, and one of the justifications for building the line, consigned just five tons of coal by rail in a year. In 1915 the locals were alarmed with the arrival one day of a railway gang to begin demolishing its rather impressive station; they were told the building was not being used and was being moved to a mainline station.

The line lasted into the 1960s due to some heavy traffic in its last years. The branch was used to rail equipment and supplies for the construction of the Roxburgh hydro dam. While the Roxburgh branch to the north actually ran to within a few kilometres of the dam site, the restricted widths of tunnels prevented the carriage on the line of over-gauge items, such as the larger components of the power station equipment, and so these were shipped to Bluff, then railed up the main line to McNab, then routed up the Waikaka branch, with a large crane being erected at the terminus of the branch to offload the heavy equipment on to trucks. The completion of the Roxburgh dam and power station removed the main justification for retaining the Waikaka branch and it closed on 9 September 1962.

Nelson Section — New Zealand's greatest railway saga

Length: 96.64 km (to Glenhope); 103.2 km (to shortlived terminus at Kawatiri). Rails were laid to Gowanbridge (109.5 km), but this section never opened to traffic and was lifted in 1942 when Glenhope again became the terminus.
Opened: 2 September 1912 (to Glenhope); 21 June 1926 (to Kawatiri),
Passenger services: Withdrawn 13 June 1954.

Status: Closed Glenhope-Kawatiri 12 July 1931; closed completely 13 June 1954; re-opened 17 June 1954; closed finally 3 September 1955.

There were almost always local protests of varying degrees of intensity when line closures were announced, but none has before or since created quite the stir as did the decision in 1955 to shut the Nelson section. The closure received national attention mainly through the actions of a group of local women who sat down on the line at Kiwi station so as to prevent work trains reaching the southern terminus at Glenhope and start lifting the rails. Local NZR officials decided to suspend demolition work; at the same time, the Nelson Provincial Progress League organised a large petition calling for the Nelson section not only to be retained, but for it to be connected to the Main North line in Marlborough. On 29 September 1955—three days after the sit-in on the line began—police arrested nine of the women at Kiwi station. While they were being taken back to Nelson, there was what the *Nelson Evening Mail* described as a 'further sensation' when the guard of the work train, named as 'Mr D. Gargiulio' announced at Kiwi that he had just resigned from NZR. After a telephone call to Nelson, a Mr Puddy was appointed acting guard and the train proceeded to Glenhope. The demolition went ahead and New Zealand's sole remaining isolated section was no more.

What price this line today? Wf 62 cuts a sad figure on this demolition train at Motupiko during March 1956, the line having
been closed to revenue traffic the year before. Motupiko was one
of just three stations on this line to be staffed. (*Derek Cross—Bob
Stott collection*)

This line was intended to run from Nelson via Murchison to tap the coal traffic from the mines of the West Coast.
The problem along the West Coast, which was the country's
most important coal supplier, was that there were no natural
harbours; instead, the colliers had to make the run in and out
of the mouths of the Grey and Buller Rivers, with all the navigational and tidal complexities involved. Nelson by contrast
had a deepwater, all-weather port on Golden Bay. The Nel-

son section reached nowhere near the West Coast; effectively it operated only as far as Glenhope, a tiny farming settlement, although rails were laid beyond that settlement toward Gowanbridge (and trains briefly ran as far as Kawatiri) and formation work was nearing Murchison, the only town of any note along the initial route. The Glenhope-Kawatiri section did not last long, being open for traffic only from June 1926 until July 1931, while the section to Gowanbridge was never used for revenue rail services.

The first section to open was between Nelson and Foxhill, the 34 km length of track being used for regular services from 31 January 1876, At its northern end, the line was extended by 1.6 km to Nelson's port in 1880. Southwards, additional sections were opened over several years, including the 900 metre Spooner's Range tunnel.

The original plan had been for the Midland Railway Co to construct the section south from Belgrove, including tunnelling through Spooner Range's, but the task fell to NZR after the company failed to meet the terms of its contract with the government.

The Nelson section at work (year ending 30 June 1913)

Passengers	10,808
Season tickets	38
Parcels	414
Horses	6

Carriages	2
Dogs	59
Cattle	4
Calves	1
Sheep	783
Chaff and lime	180 tons
Wool	8 tons
Firewood	270 tons
Timber	311 tons
Grain	593 tons
Merchandise	484 tons
Minerals	1,122 tons

Total revenue for the year: £2,129

Source: New Zealand Gazette

The Nelson section operated largely out of the public consciousness — until its last days. But in 1952 the third Royal Commission on Railways recommended closure of the line. Politicisation of the line's future followed the announcement by the National government, led by Sidney Holland, that the section would close on 13 June 1954. Close it did, but only briefly; it re-opened four days later but without its passenger service after Nelson went into an uproar over the loss of its railway.

The Nelson Progress League had obtained guarantees from local users that there would be 28,815 tons available for transport on the line the following year. At the same time, the league's submission claimed that part of the problem was that it had been some years since NZR had made any effort to generate new business on the line and, in fact, that there had been a deliberate government policy if allowing road operators to win away business from the railway by granting exemptions to the thirty mile limit (the greatest distance road operators could move freight in competition with an existing railway). The fact that the terminus at Glenhope had only a part-time caretaker meant no one at that end of the line was working to get goods consignments for the railway. The generally dilapidated condition of stations and roiling stock also worked against the railway's customer appeal.

In 1960 the Labour government, whose successful 1957 election campaign had included a promise to connect Nelson to the South Island rail network, had parliament pass the Nelson Railway Authorisation Act which provided for the construction of a 104 km line from Nelson to join the Main North track near the then small station of Grovetown, the first station north of Blenheim. Some token earthworks had been carried out by the time Labour lost the November 1960 election and the new National administration immediately ordered a stop to the work, then quickly moved to repeal the authorising act. There was some doubt at the time about the good faith of the Labour government in leaving the start of the work so late in its term; there were also those who argued that had construction begun a year or more earlier, progress would have been such by the time of the election that National might have hesitated to abandon the project. As it was, the Nelson railway row was enough to turn the Nelson parliamentary seat from safe National to safe Labour for many elections to follow.

In its latter days, the Nelson line remained New Zealand's last remaining isolated section. Equipment provided for the section was usually old and surplus to needs on other parts of the NZR system; even to the end of its days, trains operated without continuous air brakes. There were air brakes on the locomotives but on grades the guards were required to apply hand brakes on carriages and wagons before descents. It was, in essence, a nineteenth century railway that survived its period by more than fifty years.

Another picture of **Wf 62**, this time about to collect lifted sleepers. This is 1955, the locomotive had been built at Hillside workshops, Dunedin in 1910. (*Derek Cross—Bob Stott collection*)

Rails

AN INDEPENDENT
MONTHLY
MAGAZINE

*Nelson Line: Why the
doubts linger on.*

NEW ZEALAND PRICE   NTS   DECEMBER 1972

Even by 1972, with the Nelson line closed for seventeen years,
the fate of that line was still felt strongly, as this magazine cover shows. This 1951 photograph by J. L. Stitchbury shows a **Wf**
locomotive with two wagons containing sleepers attached at one
end, livestock and open wagons at the other.

Otago Central branch

Length: 236.1 km.
Opened: 11 July 1921.
Passenger services: Passenger services beyond Alexandra withdrawn 11 May 1958. Railcars withdrawn 25 April 1976. Excursion trains operate to Pukerangi and, less often, to the present terminal at Middlemarch.
Status: Wingatui-Middlemarch operates as a private tourist railway, Closed Clyde-Cromwell 13 April 1980; closed Middlemarch-Clyde 30 April 1990.

The landscape through which the Otago Central line passed is shown to advantage in this photograph, with a very long tourist train crossing the Flat Stream viaduct and heading through a short tunnel. This section of the branch had ten tunnels. (*Dunedin Railways*)

Travelling on this line was a scenic delight. Soon after leaving Dunedin, there is the spectacular Taieri Gorge, 18 km long, with the track into rock cliffs. After crossing the Wingatui viaduct, trains pass through seven tunnels and over several bridges, including the Christmas Creek and Deep Stream viaducts (15 metres and 16 metres above stream respectively), where steel girders were laid on rock pylons. Other bridges in the gorge include Machine Creek, 21-metres high and Barewood Creek, 23-metres high. The last of the tunnels is called Notches; it is in this area that the track was cut through four rock spurs and crosses four bridges in less than 300 metres. Several small stations were located through the gorge and its approaches, as the line was once the only reliable means of transport for isolated farmers. Construction methods relied mainly on backbreaking labour by the work gangs who, apart from cutting tunnels and through spurs, had to undertake dry-stone walling.

After the gorge, the trains and railcars picked up speed on the sprawling Maniototo Plain, wound down the Ida Valley. After Clyde came the final section, the trains hugging the side of the Cromwell Gorge through which the then wild Clutha River soared its way. The line would certainly be the prime contender for being designated the most picturesque train journey in New Zealand.

The Otago Central line left the Main South at Wingatui, 12 km south of Dunedin. Construction began in 1879 after several alternative routes were considered and dismissed. One of the many other proposals entertained briefly was building a line right through to Queenstown with a connection down the edge of Lake Wakatipu to Kingston and so to link with the rail line from Invercargill. Before the present route through the Taieri Gorge was settled upon, there were schemes to construct routes south from Duntroon on what would be Kurow branch, or extend the Dunback branch. There was even thought of extending the existing line into Central Otago that then terminated at Lawrence (and would later be extended to Roxburgh). None of the routes out of Dunedin offered an easy construction job given the difficult nature of the terrain between the coast and Central Otago. And even when the route was settled, the long and painful economic depression of the 1880s meant progress was made extremely slowly over several years.

It was not until 1889 that a section as far as Hindon in the Taieri Gorge (at the 26.8 km mark) was opened to traffic. Gradually, the rails inched forward, progress picking up once the gorge section was completed and the construction gangs moved to the flat terrain of the Strath Taieri. Middlemarch was reached 1891, Ranfurly in 1898, Omakau in 1901, Alexandra in 1906, Clyde in 1907 and (delayed by the First World War) Cromwell in 1921.

While day-return mixed trains were run into Dunedin from successive railheads, timetabled passenger-only trains did not start operating until 1900 (from Ranfurly and stopping at Hyde for lunch). It was not until 1928 that carriages were heated on these consists. Once the railhead became Clyde, a daily passenger train left Dunedin at 7.15 am to arrive at Clyde station at 4.30 pm; when the rails reached the planned terminus at Cromwell in 1921 another fifty minutes were added to cover that last section. All mixed trains were replaced with passenger-only trains in 1936, only for the mixed trains to make a comeback in 1951, continuing until 1956 when railcars were introduced on the line allowing connections at Dunedin with Christchurch-Invercargill expresses; the railcar arrived from Central Otago in time for its passengers to catch the Christchurch-bound express. It then waited until the Invercargill-bound service arrived and departed Dunedin before making its return journey to Cromwell. This timetable remained in place until the end of passenger services on the Otago Central line, although the Alexandra-Cromwell part of the railcar run was abolished in 1958.

Until its last years, the Otago Central line was a busy freight route. Much farm produce, including fruit from around Clyde, went down to Dunedin. In the years before fast road transport, the trains hauled fuel and fertiliser as well as the Dunedin news-paper, the Otago Daily Times, to people living in Central. The last great surge of the line's business came during the construc-tion of the Clyde hydro dam. While this meant the end of the section to Cromwell (that route now lies well under the man-made Lake Dunstan), the dam construction did sustain the re-mainder of the line for another decade.

A notable weather event happened in July 1908. A heavy snowfall, which reached a depth of about one metre at Oture-hua, caused chaos on the Otago Central line. Heavy rain and wind blew over telegraph poles near Hyde, and a foot of water in the yards there meant that the Clyde-bound express could proceed no further. A Dunedin-bound goods train became em-bedded in a snowdrift just after leaving Ida Valley station. A following mixed train was also trapped. Then, a few days later, more snow fell and a goods train was trapped near Waipiata. Two locomotives were coupled together with a snowplough in front to clear the line, but the leading engine was derailed when it hit a block of frozen snow. Days of clearing work followed before the line could be re-opened.

In April 1990 when the government announced the closure of the line, the local response was immediate. The people of Dunedin raised $1.2 million to allow the city council to buy the 63.81 km section between Middlemarch and Wingatui, making it the longest privately owned railway in New Zealand. Middlemarch has one of the few remaining examples of the New Zealand country railway station. The owners have retained the old wooden station and the typical goods shed, as well as the sidings. All that is missing are old four-wheeler wagons with their doors hanging down while being unloaded by local farmers.

Te Aro Line

Length: 1.81 km.
Opened: 27 March 1893.
Passenger services: This was primarily a passenger line and those services continued until closure. It was the introduction of electric tramways services in parallel with the line that spelled its doom.
Status: Closed on 23 April 1917.

This line ran from the government's Lambton station in Wellington, along the waterfront to near what is today the intersection of Tory and Wakefield Streets. It was closed following complaints from business people that the trains were creating a smoke nuisance, and they also objected to the noise of the locomotives and their whistles. (At one stage, the Railways Department halved the number of trains using the line, to ten movements a day, to appease the complainants.)

The building of the line to Te Aro was spurred by the fact that, in the early 1890s, both the Thorndon (Wellington & Manawatu Railway Company) and Lambton (NZR) stations were a considerable distance from those who lived in the first-established housing areas of Wellington (Te Aro Flat or on Mt Victoria; indeed, these Wellingtonians considered both the stations were 'out of town'. It was thus decided to bring the railway into the city.

After the commitment was made to build the line to Te Aro, its viability was compromised by the decision of the railway commissioners that it would be a passenger-only line, as they were opposed to having a second goods yards within the city (but trains did carry parcels and dogs on the Te Aro line). Meanwhile, the Wellington Chamber of Commerce was lobbying for the Te Aro line to be built and operated by the WMR, with both that company's and NZR trains able to use the line. In the end, it was the government railway that operated the line.

The Te Aro station consisted of three sets of tracks, two with platforms and a centre track for locomotives to reverse around their trains. The main station was 26 metres long with six rooms for NZR staff. It had separate waiting rooms for men and women and a large entrance lobby; the platforms were each 143 metres long. Traffic reached its peak in 1904, with 212 trains a week (including long distance services such as the Masterton trains and the Napier Mail), but the introduction of electric trams that year triggered a decline in rail traffic as it become more convenient and faster for people in town to jump on a tram. Ther line was made even less attractive by the fact that the trains were limited to six miles an hour (four past wharf gates). A seeming lifeline was thrown in 1912 when *The Dominion* newspaper reported that the Te Aro Railway League managed to get some of services returned to the station: the morning and evening trains to and from the Wairarapa would once again serve Te Aro rather than originating and terminating at Lambton station. The league was also agitating for a goods shed to be erected and the newspaper said the Minister of Railways, William Herries, had written to the Wellington Harbour Board seeking land to be used as a railway goods shed.

By 1916 the line was seeing just sixty-two trains a week, mostly at peak hours (although on Sundays all trains from the Hutt Valley terminated at Te Aro rather at Larmbton station, with many Wellingtonians travelling to the Hutt for picnics). The line's end came with the First World War and the introduction of new timetables in 1917 to save coal. It was decided that running trains along the Wellington waterfront could no longer be justified.

* * *

8
Vital Statistics

The savagery of the river that night is shown in the damage suffered by these carriages at Tangiwai.

Accidents

The twelve worst railway accidents in New Zealand history were:

1. Tangiwai, 24 December 1953. The 3.00 pm Wellington-Auckland express hauled by Ka 949 and consisting of nine carriages and two vans plunged into the Whangaehu River near Tangiwai, killing 151 of the 285 people aboard. A passing local motorist Cyril Ellis, realising the rail bridge had been damaged and knowing the express was due, ran down the line waving a torch; the driver saw it and applied the brakes but it was too late, the trains still travelling at such speed that the locomotive hit the banks on the other side of the river. The accident was the result of a rush of water (known as a lahar) from a breached crater lake on Mt Ruapehu hurtling down the river, the combination of water, mud and rocks severely damaging the railway bridge. Tangiwai was a small station (closed in 1986) about one kilometre south of the Whangaehu River. The express approached the bridge just after 10.20 pm, the crew unaware that the structure had damaged by a six-metre-high wall of water just thirty minutes earlier. All but three first class carriages and two vans plunged into the river bed. One carriage teetered on the edge of the bridge. Ellis and the guard, William Inglis, entered the carriage and managed to get some passengers out before the coupling snapped and it, too, plunged to the riverbed. Ellis then scrambled down and broke windows to help other passengers escape. He was awarded the George Cross.

2. Hyde, Central Otago, 4 June 1943. The Otago Central line is one of the few secondary railway routes to experience a tragedy along the lines of that which occurred Hyde at 1.45pm on 4 June 1943 in which twenty-one people died and forty-seven were injured. The express from Cromwell had passed through Hyde station itself when excessive speeds caused the passengers to be thrown around their carriages. At a cutting just south of Hyde the train left the rails and ended up a pile of twisted steel and wood. It was about ninety minutes before rescuers reached the scene. This tragedy was also unusual in that it was not the result of a natural disaster or 'Act of God', but rather of serious dereliction of duty by the driver of Ab 782 who, a board of inquiry concluded, was under the influence of alcohol when he boarded the locomotive and then had consumed more while in control. Bottles of beer were found on the engine. The inquiry further concluded the train was travelling at about 70 mp/h (or 112 km/h) at the time of the accident on a curve with a speed limit of 30 mp/h. The driver was sentenced to three years in prison for manslaughter, and the guard was reprimanded for not taking action when the train reached excessive speed.

3. Ongarue, 6 July 1923. This incident caused the first major loss of life on New Zealand's railway system. An Auckland-Wellington express on the North Island Main Trunk struck a huge landslide. In all, seventeen people were killed and twenty-eight seriously injured. The train had left Auckland at 10.50 pm and dawn was just breaking at 6.50 am on that winter morning when the train hit the landslide, the engine and postal van being derailed and the three following second-class carriages telescoped. The guard at the rear of the train was reported to have felt only a slight bump but when he realised there had been an accident he grabbed an axe and headed for the damaged carriages to help get passengers out. The debris included one large boulder weighing more than a ton. Apart from the damage caused by the impact, the gas cylinder in the third second-class carriage caught fire, but another slide of mud put out the flames before they engulfed the passengers. When news reached Taumarunui, two special trains were despatched to the scene with doctors, nurses, pharmacists, stretchers and other equipment. The bodies of the dead, along with the injured passengers, arrived back in Taumarunui at 2.00 pm on one of the special trains.

In the aftermath, there were questions why the second-class cars were always placed at the front of the train with first class and sleeper cars at the rear, and why the danger was not spread more evenly among the classes of passengers. However, it remained NZR practice until the end of steam that second class carriages were placed immediately behind the engine; it was department policy that people paying more to travel in first class were also paying to be away from the noise, coal fumes and grit produced by steam locomotives. In the Tangiwai disaster, only one first-class passenger died; the remainder of the fatalities were second-class passengers and train crew.

4. **Ratana, 26 March 1938.** A Good Friday Wellington to New Plymouth passenger train derailed in heavy fog, the driver having missed seeing a speed restriction sign. Seven people died, and another forty were injured.

5. Seddon, 25 February 1948. A Picton to Christchurch express crashed after the locomotive derailed due to the train travelling at excessive speed. Six passengers were killed and sixty-three injured. The driver was acquitted when tried for manslaughter.

6. Rakaia, 11 March 1899. Two picnic excursion trains carrying workers from the Islington freezing works and their families were involved in a collision, with one of the trains smashing into the rear of the other. Three women and one child were killed, with another twenty-two people injured.

7. Waiouru Bank, 18 August 1981. A Silver Fern railcar travelling from Wellington to Auckland was moving down the Waiouru Bank at approximately 40 km/h above the speed limit for a curve when the railcar rolled over, killing four passengers and injuring sixteen people (one seriously).

8. Mataroa, 8 November 1918. At Mataroa, just north of Taihape on the North Island Main Trunk, the train hit a large landslide. Two workers in the postal van (the second vehicle behind the locomotive) were killed, as were two passengers in the first car (the third vehicle).

9. Rimutaka Incline, 11 September 1880. Two carriages were swept from the line by gale-force winds at Siberia Curve, killing three children and injuring twenty-one passengers. NZR subsequently built a large wooden windbreak at this site to shield trains from the frequent high winds at this exposed point.

10. Rolleston, 23 August 1993. The Southerner express was struck by a loaded concrete mixer truck on a level crossing at Rolleston, on the outskirts of Christchurch. Three passengers were killed and seven seriously injured.

11. Whangamarino, 27 May 1914. A goods train was moving into the loop at this station south of Mercer when an express train crashed into its rear. Three people were killed.

12. Haywards, 8 November 1943. An Upper Hutt–Wellington suburban service travelling on the old Hutt line was derailed when the leading wheels of the locomotive left the line and carriages piled up alongside the engine. Three people were killed, twenty injured.

★ ★ ★

Bridges and Viaducts

Longest: Rakaia River. Main South line (1,744 metres)
Longest (North Island): Tauranga Harbour, East Coast Main Trunk (441 metres)
Highest: Mohaka Gorge, Palmerston North–Gisborne line (97 metres)
Highest (South Island): Staircase Gully, Midland line (73 metres)

A J class locomotive hauls a mixed train out of Riverton and across the bridge spanning the town's estuary. (*Southland Museum and Art Gallery*)

The earliest bridges and viaducts in New Zealand were often timber trestles (the Hawke's Bay line being a prime example), most of those later being replaced by steel structures. Native timbers such as totara were the obvious choice at the beginning as many of the North Island lines were constructed through areas of dense forests, so the raw materials were readily to hand; on top of that, with unstable ground and river beds to cross, timber was structurally suitable.

In parts of the South Island, though, there were no such forests. Some longer bridges in Canterbury and Otago required hardwoods imported from Australia; the Otago Central line passed largely through treeless areas, and the builders there opted for wrought iron.

At its zenith, the NZR system included more than 2,600 bridges and viaducts. Some of the longest bridges are in Canterbury, where rivers wind to the sea between wide stretches of gravel. The present bridge over the Rakaia River, with 143 spans, was built in 1939, replacing the original wooden structure.

For the traveller, a trip on the Palmerston North to Napier line offered some dramatic views; in the 19 km of track between Dannevirke and Kopua you cross six viaducts: Mangatera (25 metres high), Piri Piri (29 metres), Matamau (30 metres), Makotoku (26 metres), Ormondville (39 metres) and Kopua (29 metres).

The combined road-rail bridge was an economy measure, and was especially suited to branch lines where both train and motor vehicle traffic were light. This bridge on the Mossburn branch line in Southland was adequate even though it was on the route between the tourist centres of Lake Te Anau and Milford Sound because there were only a handful of train movements over any week. (*Derek Cross—Bob Stott collection*)

Apart from the standard road-rail bridge, there were some interesting variations. South of Blenheim the Awatere River was crossed with a shared bridge, but on two levels. Similar bridges erected on the now mothballed Okahukura section in King Country and on the now bypassed section through the Karangahake Gorge on the East Coast Main Trunk.

An unusual bridge was that constructed in 1885 at Te Aroha: it included a swing span used when vessels were plying the

Thames River. But the swing section soon was redundant: the arrival of the railway in Te Aroha cut sharply into the river shipping trade. In 1913 NZR removed the swing span and replaced it with a fixed span.

This massive concrete arch viaduct was a dominating feature of the Opunake branch in the North Island province of Taranaki. Here WW 561 heads an enthusiast's special. (*Bob Stott*)

Gradients

Steepest:
1 in 33 — Otira tunnel
1 in 35 — North of Wanganui on the Marton-New Plymouth line
1 in 35 — The Mamaku Ranges on the now mothballed Rotorua branch
1 in 36 — Johnsonville branch (Wellington suburban line)
1 in 37 — Picton to Elevation on the Main North line in the South Island

Longest:
1 in 47 over 48 km — Rolleston-Springfield, Midland line.

Tunnels

Longest:
>Kaimai, East Coast Main Trunk (8,850 metres)
>Rimutaka, Wairarapa line (8,798 metres)
>Otira, Midland Line (8,554 metres)
>Tawa No. 2, North Island Main Trunk (4,323 metres)
>Tikiwhata, Palmerston North-Gisborne (2,989 metres)
>Lyttelton, Main South line (2,595 metres)
>Turakina, New Plymouth-Marton line (2,091 metres)
>Okahukura, Stratford-Okahukura line (1,525 metres)
>Fordell, New Plymouth-Marton line (1,459 metres)
>Waikoura, Palmerston North-Gisborne (1,443 metres)

Northernmost: No. 1 tunnel, Okaihau branch (142 metres).
There was also a short tunnel built north of Okaihau on
the never completed extension from Okaihau to Rangiahua.

Southernmost: Glenham branch (301 metres)

The New Zealand terrain is such that tunnels were very much
a critical part of the country's railway construction. Some have
long been out of use as the branch lines were closed; for example, the Moutohora branch running inland from Gisborne was
closed on 24 March 1959. It had four tunnels. Others have been
'daylighted' or 'opened out'; that is, replaced by a deep cutting.
In 1965, when the branch line closures had begun and the Kaimai tunnel still not completed, the NZR system still had 189
tunnels with a total length of 86 km.

The 2,595 metre Lyttelton tunnel, which allowed the connection by rail of the port there with Christchurch on the other side of the hills, was one of the first large-scale engineering works undertaken in New Zealand, made imperative by
the lack of practical alternatives of transport between the port
and the new settlement that would grow into New Zealand's
second largest city. The first sod was turned on 17 July 1861
and, by tunnelling from both ends, the breakthrough was made
possible by 1867. The tunnel was opened to traffic on 9 November that year with the first passenger train running through
the following month. The tunnel had originally been laid to
the broad gauge then obtaining in Canterbury and in April

1876 was converted to the narrow gauge adopted as the national gauge. Electric traction was used through the tunnel between 1929 and 1970.

The Otira tunnel was opened to traffic on 4 August 1923, at which time it was the longest tunnel in what was then the British Empire. Electric power for the Otira tunnel was initially provided by a coal-fired power station, operated by NZR, until hydroelectric power became available in 1941. When Tranz Rail took over the NZR network, it decided to eliminate electric traction through the Otira tunnel as the electric locomotives were seen as being unable to handle the heavy trains expected as the coal traffic increased. Powerful fans and doors were installed along the length of the tunnel to provide ventilation, and the DX diesel-electric locomotives were fitted with modified air intake systems so that they could operate through the tunnel.

The Tawa No.2 tunnel was built as part of the Tawa Flat deviation north of Wellington, while the Tikiwhata tunnel is one of twelve tunnels in the comparatively short stretch of track between Kopuawhara and Bartletts on the Gisborne line; the tunnel at Waikoura is also located on that line. Turakina and Fordell on the Marton-New Plymouth line were built as part of the deviation opened in 1947; the 1,525 metre Okahukura tunnel is located on the line between that township and Stratford.

The opening of the Rimutaka tunnel on 3 November 1955 spelled the end of one of the most remarkable lines in the NZR system, the Rimutaka Incline. The commitment to tunnel under the Rimutaka Ranges was made as early as 1923, but the project was judged to be less urgent than the completion of the

Tawa Flat deviation on the line out of Wellington to Palmerston North. Then the Great Depression and the Second World War delayed the tunnel still further, and it was not until 1949 that preparatory work began and, finally in 1951, construction proper had started. By mid-1954 construction trains were able to traverse the full length of the tunnel. The tunnel's opening had two immediate benefits: first, it reduced train times significantly, typically shaving about two hours off a shunting goods service operating between Wellington and Masterton; secondly, it relieved congestion on the North Island Main Trunk and line through the Manawatu Gorge, as much goods traffic between the capital and Hawke's Bay could be moved via Upper Hutt and Masterton, something impossible in the days of the incline and railway over the ranges. The tunnel itself was built to sufficient height to allow for future electrification.

At the time of its construction, the Kaimai tunnel in the Bay of Plenty became the fourteenth longest tunnel in the world and the longest in the Southern Hemisphere. It was designed as the key element of the Kaimai deviation, offering a more direct route to the Bay of Plenty than the long-established one via Paeroa and Katikati. The deviation reduced the rail distance between Hamilton and Tauranga by 52 km and also allowed heavier loads to be carried because of the reduction in the average climbing grade on the route. When approved, the estimated cost of the tunnel was $11.4 million. The first sod was turned on the deviation at Apata on 2 October 1965. The construction involved the use of fifteen battery-electric and eleven diesel locomotives, along with sixty side-tipping wagons, as well as other specialised rolling stock. The tunnel was opened to traffic on 12 September 1978 and replaced the 1,006-metre Karangahake tunnel on the by now bypassed old section of the East Coast Main Trunk.

Some of the twenty-six tunnels on the North Island Main Trunk (via the Tawa Flat deviation) have been opened out over the years (particularly in advance of electrification), including the former 180 metre Makohine tunnel in 1984. The Main South line required rather fewer tunnels, there being none in Canterbury south of Christchurch nor in Southland. The longest tunnel on the line is that at Mihiwaka, 1,408 metres, as the line winds around the hills north of Dunedin. Once the track levels out on the shore of Otago Harbour, trains pass through the 313 metre Blanket Bay tunnel, which was opened on 13 June 1948, as part of the deviation between Sawyers Bay and St Leonards. After Dunedin, trains pass through the second longest tunnel, the 1,407 metre Caversham tunnel, followed by the 889 metre Chain Hills tunnel near Wingatui.

The Main North line to Picton had twenty-two tunnels, although in recent years tunnel No.22 north of Dashwood was 'daylighted' and No.4 south of Oaro was bypassed. Twenty of the tunnels were located between Claverley (where the line, after running through the interior of North Canterbury, reaches the coast with consequent spectacular views for passengers) and Clarence (not far south of the Waima River, after which the line leaves the coastline). Nine of the tunnels are contained in the relatively short distance between Goose Bay and Puketa, where trains emerge from one tunnel to run a short distance before disappearing into another.

Apart from the long Otira tunnel, the Midland line has six-teen tunnels in the 17 km between Otarama and Avoca. In the mid-1980s twelve tunnels floors on the Christchurch-Grey-mouth line were lowered to allow containers to be transported on flat wagons.

On the Wellington suburban system the short 10.49 km Johnsonville branch line includes seven tunnels, five spaced in the short distance between Wellington yards and Crofton Downs station.

Several secondary and branch lines required extensive tun-nelling. The Stratford-Okahukura line was built with twen-ty-four tunnels, with six of them located in just a 13 km stretch between Tangarakau and Heao. The Stillwater-Westport line includes six tunnels, one north of Tawhai and the remainder in the Buller Gorge. The Otago Central line had thirteen tun-nels, ranging from Salisbury at 437 metres to Machine Creek, 55 metres, both still in use as part of the tourist railway that operates trains on the remaining section of the line to the new railhead at Middlemarch. Further south, the Roxburgh branch had three tunnels, two of them located on the stretch of tight curves and difficult grades through the Manuka Gorge. Other branches requiring tunnels were Moutohora (four), Rewanui (two), Tokarahi, Tapanui and Catlins River (one each); the spur line into the wharves at Port Chalmers passes through a short tunnel underneath part of the township to emerge on the wa-terfront. The Nelson section had the 900 metre Spooners Range tunnel, which was completed on 14 June 1893 and closed when the line ceased operating on 5 September 1955.

Appendix:
Railway Heritage

A book published in 1982 showed just quick enthusiasts were off the mark at the end of the steam era in trying to preserve as many types of locomotives — along with by then redundant rolling stock — as was possible. Neill Cooper's Preserved NZR Locomotives and Railcars issued that year shows that, by 1982, almost seventy steam locomotives, four electric locomotives, one diesel-electric locomotive, a few diesel shunters and tractors and nine railcars had been acquired for preservation.

Fortunately, as Cooper pointed out, many smaller locomotives had, after finishing their working lives with New Zealand Railways, been sold off to the Public Works Department, quarries, coal mines, sawmills, cement works, freezing works and private railways, saving them from the scrapyard. These included the A class 0-4-0T, the D class 2-4-0T, along with some engines in the C class 0-4-2T and F class 0-6-0T. As his book shows, the first phase was to use old engines as static displays in parks where, inevitably, they were at the mercy of the elements such as the case, for example, of the Fell which had been used on the Rimutaka Incline ending up in the middle of the grass park in Featherstone.

But then locomotives started to be acquired in working condition or capable of being restored to working condition, and it was these small industrial engines that formed the backbone of the Ocean Beach Railway in Dunedin when that project was begun in 1960. By 1963, the Ferrymead Historical Park project was to be the destination for other F class locomotives.

Then came the Glenbrook Vintage Trust, which acquired part of the closed Waiuku branch, and Steam Incorporated at Paekakariki which aimed higher (or, at least, bigger), looking for Ja and K class locomotives as they were retired from main line running. The Glenbrook trust emerged from the Railway Enthusiasts' Society and it garnered a lot of early attention through the movement to its site of its first steam locomotives. The initial trip in May 1969 of Ww 480, a 4-6-4T class tank locomotives from the West Coast, created a great of media coverage at the time. This was followed by the moving of South Island-based Ja 1250. The engine was attached at Wellington to a consist of five cars, a bogie coal wagon and guard's van for what was called the South Pacific Steam Safari, an Easter excursion in 1972 that went via Upper Hutt, the Rimutaka tunnel, Woodville, the Manawatu Gorge, then on via Marton and New Plymouth, the Stratford-Okahukura line, a side trip over the Raurimu Spiral, and thence to Auckland, 1107 km in all. The special features of this journey included the first time a 'live' steam engine had been through the Rimutaka tunnel (although a Da class diesel was doing all the work) and it was the first South Island Ja ever to run in the North Island.

The closure of the Fairlie branch (from the junction at Washdyke) in Canterbury triggered the formation of the Pleasant Point Railway and Historical Society, while the Ashburton Railway and Preservation Society eyed part of the 43.1 km Mount Somers branch line (leaving the main line at Tinwald). The Ashburton operation today is better known as the Plains Vintage Railway and Museum. It bought the section from the junction with the Main South line to Frasers Road, and then leased land in the Tinwald Domain for its headquarters. The station from Chertsey on the Main South was moved to the site. The museum is possibly best known for its Rogers K class locomotive, K88, which was returned to steam after having been buried in the Oreti River in Southland for forty-seven years. When the 2-4-2 locomotive was recommissioned in November 1972, it was accurately termed one of the world's most remarkable locomotive restoration projects. The engine, which had originally borne the name Washington, was built for New Zealand Railways by the Rogers Locomotive and Machine Works of New Jersey in 1878. It was decommissioned in 1926 and, along with more than a dozen other locomotives, was later dumped in the Oreti to protect a railway embankment near Branxholme station.

K 88 was retrieved from the river in 1974 looking, as was described later, 'an absolute wreck'. After a good deal of debate locally as to what would be done with the remains of the engine, it was the Ashburton society that came to the rescue. Once it had been transported to Tinwald, the first months were spent washing the mud out of the engine. Fortunately for the success of the venture, tests showed the boiler was sound, as was the firebox. Over the next years, original Rogers parts were found and, when they weren't, were made. Most of the machining work was carried out at an Ashburton firm, with help also from the Hillside workshops in Dunedin.

But many prizes had disappeared by the time these pioneering groups sprang to life. No motive power from the Wellington and Manawatu Railway Company exists today. All the Q class locomotives went to the wreckers' yards, as did many of the A and Ab classes, although thankfully some were spared — particularly the two Ab engines that were saved under the enlightened watch of Railways Minister Peter Gordon for use on the Kingston Flyer.

A few early motive power examples survived. The Otago Settlers' Museum, just next to the Dunedin Railway station, and placed behind glass both ends of the steam spectrum: from 1872, Josephine, the Double Fairlie and, beside it, Ja 1274, the last steam locomotive to be built at the Hillside workshops in the city. Preservation of the latter locomotive was the idea of the Otago Branch of the New Zealand Railway and Locomotive Society and kicked off the fund raising with two 'Farewell to Steam' excursions to Palmerston as well as a raffle; altogether, $1,900 was raised, added to by the sale of mock share certificates in the locomotive (another $4,000).

In the ensuing decades, railway preservation in New Zealand has become increasingly ambitious. Typical of this trend was the formation in 1982 of the Weka Pass Railway with plans to restore part of the Waiau brand line in North Canterbury. The branch was originally 66.55 km in length, but the group's eyes were just on the 14.7 km section from the Main North line at Waipara to the second station along the branch, Waikari (the intermediate stop having been Frog Rock). One of the earliest acquisitions was the purchase in 1986 of the station building from Mina to be relocated at the Waipara end of the line, and then was renamed Glenmark.

As well as the loss of locomotives and other rolling stock, those in charge of the New Zealand railway system showed an unlikely enthusiasm for demolition of fine railway stations that today would be valued local heritage items.

Some 12.8 km of the old Waiau branch in North Canterbury was purchased by the Weka Pass Railway to operate as a tourist railway. The group now has a range of rolling stock, and its a 428 is seen here hauling one of the regular trains. The locomotive was built in 1909 by A & C Price of Thames in the North Island, and is the only A class locomotive in operating condition. (*Weka Pass Railway*)

K88, 'Washington', was built in 1877 by Rogers Locomotive Works of Paterson, New Jersey, and shipped to New Zealand for service in the South Island, becoming the first American loco-motive imported by New Zealand. Initially, this locomotive was used on expresses between Christchurch and Dunedin but when trains became longer and heavier, K 88 was transferred to branch duties and ended its days on the Waimea Plains line in South-land. When it was withdrawn in the 1920s, the locomotive was dumed in the Oreti River as flood protection. It was discovered in 1972 and then followed years of painstaking restoration at the Plains Vintage Railway near Ashburton, where it operates today. (*Roy Sinclair*)

* * *

Acknowledgements

Once again, Bob Stott came to the rescue with key photographs from his collection. Bob and I founded Rails magazine in 1971. After four years, I went off to other pursuits and Bob and his wife Jan kept the magazine going into the twenty-first century — a remarkable achievement.

I am grateful, too, to both Wilson Lythgoe and Roy Sinclair. I discovered Wilson's photographs on the internet and he was happy to supply some of his great photos: including the cover shot taken at Milton. His travels throughout New Zealand resulted in a rich portfolio capturing the last years of steam and many lines, including one in this book of Lake Omapere Road Crossing station very much on its last legs. Roy Sinclair answered my cry for help to fill several gaps and provided some wonderful photographs.

Thanks to Euan McQueen for allowing me a cartographic shortcut by the reproduction of maps he drew for his Rails in the Hinterland, New Zealand's Vanishing Railway Landscape (Grantham House 2005) which offers a large helping of nostalgia with evocative photographs of scenes no longer with us.

Others to help out with pictures were Bryan Blanchard and Jason Durry, two of the stalwarts of the preservation movement, as well as Wairarapa Archive, Alexander Turbull Library,

Horowhenua Historical Trust, Southland Museum and Art Gallery and Weka Pass Railway.

Bibliography

Periodicals

New Zealand Railway Observer
New Zealand Railfan
New Zealand Railways Magazine
Rails
(In addition, local newspaper accounts have been widely used.)
Le Rossignol, James Edward and Downie Stewart, William, "Railways in New Zealand", *The Quarterly Journal of Economics*, Vol. 23, No. 4, August 1909.

Books

Alexander, R.B., *The Stratford-Okahukura Line*, NZ Railway and Locomotive Society, 1961 and 1983
Barber, Laurie, *Frontier Town: A History of Te Awamutu 1884-1984*, Ray Richards/Te Awamutu Borough Council, 1984
Black, Henry William Robert, *The Mt Hutt District: Historical Record of Effort and Advance 1879-1929*, Mt Hutt Road Board 1929
Britten, Rosemary, *Between the Wind and the Water: Ashburton County 1876-1989*, Ashburton District Council, 1991

Churchman, Geoffrey B., *The Wellington to Johnsonville Railway*, Industrial Publishing, 1988

— *The Golden Era of Fiat Railcars in New Zealand*, IPL Books, 1989

— *The Midland Line*, Industrial Publishing, 1989

Cooper, N.J., *Preserved NZR Locomotives and Railcars*, NZRLS, 1982

Conly, Geoff and Stewart, Graham, *New Zealand Tragedies on the Track*, Grantham House 1986

Dangerfield, J.A., *Dunedin's Matchbox Railway*, NZRLS, 1986

Dangerfield J.A. and Emerson, G.W., *Over the Garden Wall: Story of the Otago Central Railway,* Otago Railway and Locomotive Society, 1995

Hoy, D.G., *Rails out of the Capital*, NZRLS, 1970

Hurst, Tony, *The Otago Central Railway: A Tribute*, IPL Books, 1990

Leitch, David B., *Railways of New Zealand*, David & Charles, 1972

Leitch, David and Scott, Brian, *Exploring New Zealand's Ghost Railways*, Grantham House, 1995

Leitch David and Stott, Bob, *New Zealand's Railways: The First 125 Years,* Heinemann Reed, 1988

McClare, E.J., *Auckland's Railway Workshops*, NZRLS, 1998

McKinnon, Malcolm (Ed), New Zealand Historical Atlas, David Bateman, 1997

Mahoney, J.D, *Down at the Station: A Study of the New Zealand Railway Station*, Dunmore Press, 1987

McGavin, T.A., *A Century of Railways in Auckland*, NZRLS, 1974

McGavin, T.A., *A Century of Railways in Marlborough*, NZRL 1977

McGavin, T.A., *A Century of Railways in Taranaki*, NZRLS 1975

McGavin, T.A., *Dunedin and Port Chalmers Railway*, NZRLS, 1973

McKinnon, Malcom et al, *Bateman New Zealand Historical Atlas*, Bateman, 1997

Meyer, R.J., **Coaling From the Clouds**, NZRLS, 1989

Orr, Russell, *The Hawke's Bay Railway*, Southern Press, 1974

Roberts, T.K., *A Compendium of Railway Construction, Part two: North Island Main Trunk* and *Part Three: Nelson and the West Coast Region*, NZRLS, 1990 and 1998

Stott, Bob, Kaimai. *The Story of Kaimai Tunnel and East Coast Main Trunk Railway*, Southern Press, 1978

— *North Island Main Trunk, 75th Anniversary Album*, Southern Press, 1983

—*The Rimutaka Incline, Yesterday and Today*, Southern Press, 1984

Troup, Gordon (Ed), *Steel Roads of New Zealand. An Illustrated Survey*, A.H. & A.W. Reed, 1973

Wilkinson, Doug, *Wellington's First Railway*, Southern Press, 1974

Woods, Chris, *Steaming to the Sunrise: A history of railways in the Gisborne region*, IPL Books, 1996

Wright, Matthews, *New Zealand's Engineering Heritage 1870-2000*, Reed Books, 1999

OTHER BOOKS
BY ROBIN BROMBY
(and available at Amazon):

Australian Railways: Their Life and Times

The nightmare of three different gauges, the daunting challenge of building railways across vast open spaces often with no water supplies, the follies of railway lines that were rarely used—all this is the saga of Australian railways, the sheer hard work and suffering of those who gave their life in service to the railways. Brimming with anecdotes and colorful stories, Australian Railways: Their Life and Times documents the old, the odd and the now forgotten. Complete with rare historic photographs.

Fighting on Empty: How Hitler and Hirohito Lost the Economic War

Nazi Germany, Imperial Japan and Fascist Italy all embarked on their Second World War plans of conquest without one vital factor: sound economies that could absorb and withstand the stresses of total war. In this groundbreaking study, Robin Bromby shows how all three Axis powers went into battle with seriously flawed economies, inadequate industrial capacity and deficient food security. When they invaded much of Europe and East Asia, the Nazis and their partners only compounded the problem: they had made few plans to manage their conquests and failed to harness captured factories and farms.

It was a fatal flaw: their war plans were doomed. Despite the legend of a beleaguered Britain, that country was the largest economy in Europe and was soon building more aircraft than Germany – and had its empire on which to call. Japan's lack of economic planning was breathtaking and the strains soon began to show. And then came the Americans with all their economic power. The Axis was finished.

Fighting on Empty reveals a largely ignored, but crucial, aspect of the Second World War.

German Raiders of the South Seas: The extraordinary true story of naval deception, daring and disguise 1914-1917

Fat from the mud and slaughter of the Western Front, there was another face of the Great War — an oddly stirring and thrilling one, characterised by chivalry and remarkably few casualties. This is the story of how three German naval surface raiders disrupted British shipping across large swathes of the Indian and Pacific oceans between 1914 and 1917. Critical cargoes and much needed reinforcements for the trenches in France and Belgium were hamstrung by German daring on the high seas.

Were it not all real and true, it would make wonderful fiction: the buccaneering crew of the Emden casting a shadow of fear over an ocean; the survivors of the battle with the Sydney sailing a leaking copra schooner from the Cocos Islands to the East Indies, the captain of the Seeadler, von Luckner, sailing a small boat halfway across the Pacific to Fiji, and then later making a dramatic escape from a New Zealand prisoner of war camp.

In the first days of World War I a German light cruiser detached itself from the East Asiatic Squadron with the mission to raid and harass Allied shipping. The ship, SMS Emden, not only became world famous in its two months of raiding, during which it sank sixteen ships and captured others, but demonstrated the vulnerability of Australian, New Zealand and Empire shipping links.

The Farming of Australia: A saga of backbreaking toil and tenacity

This is the story of triumph over a dry, hot and often infertile land. Australia's farmers have overcome difficult terrain and the tyranny of distance to make the country an important food bowl. This is the story of 200-plus years of ups and downs - savage droughts and daunting challenges but also the triumphs of irrigation and imagination and inventiveness.

The Mining Investor's Handbook: What you will need to know for the next bull market

Global bank HSBC says the metals super-cycle is still more "super" than "cycle". Deutsche Bank says metal prices will on average trend higher than over the past 40 years because they will cost much more to extract from the ground in future. JP Morgan sees the present bull cycle lasting until 2028. The Mining Investor's Handbook by newspaper commodity columnist

Robin Bromby offers some timely, and cautionary, history to the greatest commodity boom ever seen, examines the extraordinary changes that have occurred in the commodity markets — and suggests that the story is a long, long way from being played out.

All titles available in both e-format and paperback (except The Mining Investor's Handbook, which is e-format only)

Go to www.highgatepublishing.com.au for further details and free extracts from all titles.

Index

I

X ____

Y ____

Z ____

CONTINUED

You didn't promise that it would be easy

You didn't promise that I would always be happy

You did promise that you would always be there

You did promise that You wouldn't put anymore on me than I could bear

Just when I thought i couldn't make it anymore

You showed Yourself true

I exclaimed freedom before but now I'm free and living life more abundantly

Once the true freedom is attained

It is quite easy to grow in it day by day

TARA T TATE

You've untangled me from the web of human deceit

The one that says earning freedom is key

You've set me free to lie down in green pastures and to wander
beside still waters

You have restored my soul and I revel in you tender mercies anew

I want for nothing You are my portion

My eyes are set on Your Kingdom and now I know no thing, no
man, and no wickedly devised plan will keep me from it

Tara's Tater Salad

Servings | Prep Time | Total Time

SHOPPING LIST	Ingredients
Red Skin Potatoes	4 cups Red Skin Potatoes
Red Onion	¼ cup Red Onion finely chopped
Green Pepper	¼ cup Green Pepper finely chopped
Eggs	5 boiled eggs finely chopped
Turkey Bacon	6 slices Turkey Bacon crispy
Mayonnaise (Duke's)	1 ¼ cups Mayonnaise
Paprika	1 teaspoon Paprika
Italian Seasoning	½ teaspoon Italian Seasoning
Nature's Seasoning	3 teaspoons Nature's Seasoning
Black Pepper	½ teaspoon fresh Ground Black Pepper

Directions

Soak potatoes with skin on in solution of 1 cup white vinegar and 3 cups water. Scrub potatoes until no dirt or debris is on the potatoes. Cut potatoes into cubes with skin on. Place potatoes in large pot and cover with water. Cook potatoes until tender but not mushy about 20 minutes.

Bake turkey bacon in 400 degree oven for about 15 minutes on baking sheet until crispy.

Pour water off potatoes and set aside while making the seasoned mayonnaise. Place mayonnaise, paprika, Italian seasoning, Nature's Seasoning, and black pepper in the bowl that will contain the potato salad.

Add green peppers and onions to mayonnaise mixture and stir until combined. Add eggs and stir until combined. Add potatoes to mixture and stir until combined. Taste and add more Nature's Seasoning and black pepper to taste (cayenne pepper if desired).

Add chopped turkey bacon on top. Serve immediately or refrigerate.

Gail's Comfort Soup

Servings | Prep Time | Total Time

SHOPPING LIST	**Ingredients**
Onion	½ medium Onion
Ground Beef (Stew Meat)	1 pound Ground Beef (Stew Meat if available)
V8 Juice	1 (24 ounce) can pureed tomatoes
Cream of Celery Soup	1 can Cream of Celery Soup
Diced Tomatoes	2 (8 ounce) cans Diced Tomatoes
Mixed Frozen Vegetables	1 package mixed frozen Vegetables (carrots, peas, green beans, etc.)
Bay Leaf	1 Bay Leaf

Directions

Sautè onion and meat in a Dutch Oven. Cook until meat is done. Add soup, juice, and diced tomatoes; cook until boiling. Add frozen vegetables and bay leaf. Simmer until the vegetables are warmed through. The stew is best when simmered all day. Transfer from Dutch Oven to Crock Pot if desired. Keep setting on low.

Grandma's Sweet and Sour Chicken

Servings | Prep Time | Total Time

SHOPPING LIST	Ingredients
Soy Sauce	1 cup Soy Sauce
Garlic Powder	1 teaspoon Garlic Powder
White Vinegar	1/3 cup White Vinegar
Sugar	1 cup Sugar
Pepper	1 teaspoon Pepper
	8-10 Chicken Wings or 6-8 Chicken Thighs or 4 Chicken Breasts

Direction

Preheat oven to 350 degrees

Place chicken in 9x13 baking dish

Bake for 1 hour and 45 minutes frequently turning the chicken as it bakes

COLETTE'S FAVORITE POUND CAKE

Servings | Prep Time | Total Time

SHOPPING LIST	Ingredients
Cream Cheese	8 oz Cream Cheese
Eggs	6 Large Eggs
Sugar	3 cups Sugar sifted
Vanilla Extract	3 teaspoons Vanilla Extract
Lemon Extract	2 teaspoons Lemon Extract
Cake Flour	3 cups Cake Flour (All-Purpose Flour if sifted really well)
Baking Powder	$\frac{1}{2}$ teaspoon Baking Powder

Direction

Cream together butter and cream cheese

Add in 3 eggs one at a time mixing for 1 minute after each egg

Mix in half of the sugar until combined

Add in the rest of the sugar mixing well

Add the other 3 eggs on at a time mixing for 1 minute after each egg

Mix in the vanilla extract and the lemon extract

Add in half the flour and baking powder

Mix well then mix in the rest of the flour

Spoon the batter into a greased and floured bundt pan

Swirl a knife in the batter to release air

Place into oven and turn the oven to 325. Do not preheat the oven with this recipe

Bake for 1 ½ hours. Baking time may vary depending on your oven.

Let cool, remove from pan and serve

Printed in the USA
CPSIA information can be obtained
at www.ICGtesting.com
JSHW012116041124
72817JS00037B/747